JERUSALEM

Rushing toward the midnight hour

D1377946

ROBERT SMITH

JERUSALEM

Rushing Toward the Midnight Hour

Published by 21st Century Press

Springfield, MO 65807

ISBN 0-9749811-1-7

Cover: Lee Fredrickson and Keith Locke
Book Design: Terry White

Visit our web-site at: 21stcenturypress.com
and 21centurybooks.com

For childrens books visit: sonshippress.com
and sonshipbooks.com

21ST CENTURY
PRESS
PUBLISHING WITH PURPOSE
WWW.21STCENTURYPRESS.COM

DEDICATION TO:

The Jewish people who, with *Sinai in their soul*, and the *memory of the Shekinah burning in their hearts*, are forcing a wayward world to again come to grips with the eternal design of our existence. And to the Glorious Church of Jesus Christ who, upon completing its great commission to go into all the world, and along with the Jewish faithful, await the coming of the great God of our salvation, The Messiah and Lord Jesus Christ

TABLE OF CONTENTS

PREFACE

FASCINATING AND FANTASTIC TIMES

Never have we lived in more exciting and fascinating times.

Never has prophecy been more fascinating or its fulfillment more fantastic. That's why I call it FANTASTIC PROPHECIES FOR FASCINATING TIMES.

Do you believe in signs? You certainly better believe in signs. When the sign says, "STOP," that's what you had better do. Jesus challenged us to "discern the signs of the times" . . .That is what we hope to do in these writings.

Always, and in any age, there has been its share of fulfilled prophecies. The BIBLE records virtually thousands of them, but never has there been so many of them fulfilled as today.

Because most (if not all) prophecy reflects God's plans for the final revelation of his Son and the setting up of the eternal kingdom. The RETURN OF ISRAEL back to the LAND is so much a part of His final agenda. We find in these last days most of the attention of prophecy centers in the Holy Land and Jerusalem, especially as it concerns the Temple Mount. I have correctly said many times that Israel is God's time clock. We may watch the events unfold in the Middle East and easily "discern" the times. Every event in the Middle East today is a direct and clear fulfillment of the prophecies of the BIBLE.

. . . .

For 2580 years now, ever since Babylon ransacked Jerusalem and destroyed the temple, the Jews have pined for and longed for their return back. The glory of God and of Israel has never returned, although a second temple was built and remained until destroyed by Titus and the 10th army of Rome in AD 70. With the glory of God departed, the land has been under Gentile control since that fateful day in 586 BC when Nebuchadnezzar came down.

At least 2/3 of the prophecies deal with the final return of the Jews from a worldwide Diaspora, when they would repossess their land and city. Most of God's promises are prophecies that are projected to that same time. Therefore, in order to understand God's plan, we must watch carefully the events in the Middle East.

. . . .

Hal Lindsey, a very well known prophecy teacher and writer, quoted Joseph de Coursey Jr., editor in Chief of the Intelligence Digest as saying:

"I've come to the conclusion that what is happening in the Middle East is going to bring the world to it's LAST BATTLE. I know nothing about the BIBLE. I draw my conclusion from data we gather for the Digest."

The Intelligence Digest is read by over 70 of the world's Heads of State. Mr. de Coursey Jr. and Hal Lindsey are to co-author a book and I understand Lindsey has agreed.

I have personally identified over 3200 scriptural verses that are being fulfilled, or have been fulfilled in my lifetime. That's why I spend so much time studying prophecy. I find in the headlines marking current events today, that so much prophecy is being fulfilled.

There is a definite connection between God's faithfulness in keeping his word to Abraham and his seed, and

God's faithfulness to you and me. For if God cannot back up His Word today, and keep his promises to Abraham and Israel, how may I trust Him with His promises to me. If He can move the whole world of nations to bring about his word to Abraham, then I can certainly trust Him to keep His Word to me. He has promised me an ETERNAL CITY IN AN ETERNAL HEAVEN. PTL

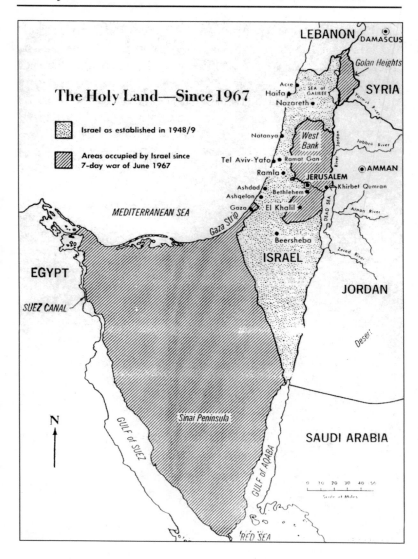

The Holy Land—Since 1967

Israel as established in 1948/9

Areas occupied by Israel since 7-day war of June 1967

INTRODUCTION

MY PURPOSE IN THIS WRITING

My purpose in this writing is certainly not to raise undo alarm. To the contrary, what I have to share should be of great comfort to the Christian (I Thessalonians 4:18). I am not interested in impressing you with knowledge, or confusing you with excess information. I do want you, however, to see the faithfulness of our God, and by seeing the faithfulness of the Lord to his prophetic word, be encouraged to put your full trust in Him. I am also interested in preparing you for an important journey that all believers in Christ will soon take. One in which we will be swept up to meet the Lord in the air.

OUR OUTLINE FOR THIS STUDY

In this study we will examine some of those fantastic prophecies, especially as they pertain to the state of Israel, the city of Jerusalem, the state of Jordan, and the West Bank. Specifically, I would like to deal with the recent Peace Treaties between Israel, the PLO, and the State of Jordan. We will try to acquaint you with the basics of the Jerusalem Covenant, which was circulated among world Jewry for ratification in 1996. Also, our study must include the Oslo Accords, Camp David, Wye, the treaty with King Hussien of Jordan and the State of Israel, and last of all, the Road Map and its prophetic significance, and why we believe only agreements with Jordan will hold. Finally we would like to talk about final judgment in the Middle East, and how God will wind up all of these events at the end of this age.

We have said that Israel is God's time clock for these final days of this age. The prophets were most concerned about the final plan for Jerusalem, the Temple Mount, and the Promised Land of Israel. Most of them prophesied near the time of the Babylonian captivity. That particular time marked the invasion of Palestine by Nebuchadnezzar, the sacking of the city of Jerusalem and the destruction of the first Temple built nearly 400 years earlier. Most influential Jews were transported to Babylon, and Settlers (or more perfectly, Colonizers) were transferred into the land of Israel to "occupy" the land. That "occupation" was to last until the end of time, when God was to restore the land, people, city and Temple. As the prophets expressed their heartbreak and sorrow for the loss of land, city and Temple at the invasion of Babylon, they were encouraged by prophetic vision which revealed an end time return of the people to the land. It was seen that they would build a second Temple at the end of 70 years. However, they were also told that in 490 years the Temple would be destroyed again, followed by a long dispersion of the people among the nations of the world. In the latter times however, this scattering of the people, and destruction of the city of Jerusalem and the Temple, would again come to an end, and the people, city, Temple, and land would be restored for a final time.

It was this greater last day's fulfillment and final return that consumes most of the prophetic writings. A time when the "occupation" of the land by Gentile powers would finally come to a complete end, and all of God's plan and promises to Abraham and his seed could finally be completely realized.

Daniel, (who was just a boy when he and his family were transported to Babylon) grew to be recognized as an especially gifted, godly man. He was made head over all the King's wise men, but his great love and concern was always for the homeland, the city and Temple in Jerusalem. He was given a vision, known as the 70 weeks vision, which foresaw a 7-year period in the end of days, hyphened by a 7-year "covenant." This covenant was to signal the day when; (l) Jerusalem would be rebuilt and set as capital of Israel; (2) The transgressions in the land would be ended; (3) The end of all sin would come; (4) Reconciliation for all iniquity would come; (5) All of the entire prophetic visions would be fulfilled; and (6) Messiah the Prince would be anointed as King over the whole world (Daniel 9:23-27).

This Covenant would be "broken" in the middle of that 7-year period, and a terrible transgression would be committed, such as would be abominable in God's sight and in the sight of all Israel.

Although many have related this "covenant" to the past and present peace treaties of Israel, we are not inclined to do so. It is true that the coming "Antichrist" will make use of the peace effort as is shown in at least three different scriptures. However, the "Covenant" in Daniel 9 seems to relate more to certain conditions concerning Jerusalem and its final day than it does to any peace process. This is not to say that the Peace Treaties are not significant in Israel. Let us discuss those treaties and their significance now, and later return to the "Covenant" of Jerusalem.

It is the author's hope that these discussions will not only be fascinating exercises in the Holy Scriptures, but will also be an inspiration of Holy living in preparation for the Lord's Coming (I John 3:3).

CHAPTER 1

JUGGLING FOR PEACE IN THE MIDDLE EAST

WHY IT WON'T WORK

It was 1962, and John F. Kennedy was our President. His assassination was but a few months away. It was summertime, but winter in the hearts of most Americans. Along with the world, our nation was sitting on the edge of its seat. Russia had been shipping missiles to Cuba. America had discovered the plot to put ballistic missiles only 90 miles from our shore, and our President was in a standoff with Michael Gorbachev. It was called the "Cuban Crisis."

Here were the world's Super Powers in a face-down, each having enough atomic power at its disposal to destroy the world several times over. The proverbial "button" could be pushed at any time, catapulting us over the brink into all-out conflict. A conflict, which would surely carry Armageddon, proportions.

Along with my pastoral duties in a small town in the

15

west, I was engaged in the building business to supplement income and to pay for a new church building we had just completed. A real-estate broker, with whom I had been working, had become very close to me. She and her husband had been most kind to the church and myself.

On the very day of the heights of the crisis, all America and particularly our city, had almost shut down, staying glued to the TV. Everyone was expecting at any minute to hear the impending doom. I was approaching the real estate office from the bank, just a block or so down the street. On this particular morning, although I was very much aware of the rest of the town's state of mind, my heart was light, and I was singing and whistling as I approached. I had just started up the front steps, when the door burst open and my friend, the real estate broker appeared. Her outburst so startled me for the moment that I stood with one foot propped on the first step.

"Reverend," she demanded, "what in the world are you so happy about? How can you be so light when the world is about to be destroyed at any minute?" I quickly regained my composure when I realized it was not a personal affront. "Well I guess I am happy because the same God who controlled my life yesterday is the same God who holds tomorrow," I said. "Besides that, I also am confident that this is not Armageddon, or the end of the world. The world is not going to blow up over Cuba." She seemed to become more relaxed. "How do you know that," she asked. By now I realized that the Lord and I were in control of the situation. "I know it because the Bible tells me so." I affirmed. "Does the Bible have something to say about the

Cuban Crisis?" she asked. My answer was a further revelation to her. "No, but it does tell us a lot about the circumstances surrounding the real battle of Armageddon,
and the end of this age. By what it tells me, I know the
end will not come over Cuba, Korea, Laos, Berlin, or any
other of all these hot spots that our world is experiencing.
But when we see the Armies of the Nations gathering in
the Middle East, and the world on edge during a
Jerusalem stand off, then we will know it is the end."

I was absolutely taken back by her response. "Please
come in and tell us about it. We need to hear this." With
that she preceded me through the door into the reception
area of her office complex. We were facing a host of
employed personnel as well as customers who all seemed
to be a bit perplexed by her outburst and our subsequent
conversation. Her announcement to the group again
startled me. "Please forgive my actions at this time, but
with the tenseness of the present situation, it is not con-
ducive to good business. I am shutting down the office
for a little while. I am going to ask the Reverend to teach
us the source of his confidence, and share with us his
knowledge of the Bible as it concerns these crises. If the
customers are pleased you may stay, or come back later,
my employees will stay and remain on the payroll." To my
utter amazement, all stayed, the doors of all the offices
were thrown open, and all were breathlessly awaiting my
words.

For the next hour I was glad to share with them much
of Bible foresight, and its predictions for the end time.
Mainly, my concentration was on the final scenario, when

the world would be at its real crisis. I did not have a Bible in hand, but through years of careful research, had most of the verses in mind. I proceeded to show that the real and final crisis would come, when the Armies of the Nations would gather in the Middle East. It slightly amazes me now, but part of my discussion speculated that the first experiment with a worldwide army would come to fruition over a crisis concerning "Babylon," which is present day Iraq. The Gulf War brought this very situation into sharp perspective. Little could I know this, except that nearly half of all the scriptures relating to the "Armies of the Nations" were in the context of "Babylon." It would be Saddam Hussein's madness that would perpetrate the "Multi national forces" and bring them to the Middle East. I shared how that eventually they would surround Jerusalem, bringing about the real "stand-off."

The above-related incident took place in August of 1962, about 43 years ago now. Today we see that very scenario in the making, as our headline News daily calls our attention to terror coming out of the Middle East. Saddam Hussein's regime has been overthrown and still we see the terrorist threat continuing. The focus is Israel, and even now little hope is extended for settling the situation in Israel and the Middle East without eventually putting "Coalition Troops" around Jerusalem. We were able to get rid of the Berlin Wall and now a partition wall is being built between the West Bank and Israel.

How perfectly accurate we can be if we stick to God's word. How perfectly calm our hearts will be as we face the crises today, knowing that the same God who has been watching over His Word to fulfill it, is the one who holds the present and future in his plans.

A SURE WORD OF PROPHECY

Nothing so establishes the truth and trustworthiness of God's Word like the fantastic way its prophecies is being fulfilled so accurately today, and in such specific detail. We have a sure word of prophecy, to which we would do well to take heed during this present age of darkness: II Peter 1:19-21 gives us this admonition:

We have also a more sure word of prophecy; whereunto ye do well that ye take heed, as unto a light that shineth in a dark place--

Jesus assures us that:
Heaven and earth shall pass away, but my word shall not pass away.

Those two scriptures are found in II Peter 1:19, and Matthew 5:18 respectively.

We are told in Isaiah 46:l0:
I am God--declaring the end from the beginning, and from ancient times the things that are not yet done.

And again in Habakkuk 2:3:
For the vision is yet for an appointed time, but at the end it shall speak, and not lie; though it tarry, wait for it; because it will surely come, it will not tarry.

Everything the Lord will do has been revealed to the

prophets in the past (Amos 3:7).

Thousands of prophesied events down through the ages were fulfilled to the letter. Can we not then fully expect all of the future prophecies to be fulfilled?

...unto them that look for him shall he appear the second time without sin unto salvation (Hebrews 9:28).

Again we are encouraged to look for Him: "Our conversation (life style) is from Heaven, from whence also we look for the Savior, the Lord Jesus Christ."

Jesus then warns us not to get so entangled with the cares of this life, so as to let that day come on us unawares (Luke 21:34).

SETTING UP THE SCENARIO FOR TODAY'S CRISIS

Comedian Clark Brown said: Friends come and go, but enemies accumulate. That is certainly true, especially for the tiny State of Israel. No matter how hard Israel tries to appease her enemies, and convince her friends, her friends wonder and vacillate back and forth, while her enemies just keep accumulating. What's new? It has always been so. Even for the Israel of the Bible.

It seems always for the Jew, no matter how many Holocausts, how many pogroms and Inquisitions, which is forced upon them, the world can never learn. Still and again Anti-Semitism will raise its ugly head. Even in a world where tolerance and good will toward all ethnic is demanded in every part of the international society, those same people who will not tolerate inhumane intolerance any where else, or for any other people, cannot find it in their hearts to seriously stem the tides of anti-Jew and anti-Israel expressions among the nations.

And that tide has not changed since the birth of the State of Israel. Thinking that a homeland and a State of their own would give the Jew a legitimate place in the world free from persecution, Britain, and the League of Nations made plans for the State of Israel. The UN and the world community followed suit. The powerful United States also gave it's backing as did the Soviet Union. Powerful money interests in the international finance and corporate arena also gave their support. With all this backing, it would appear that finally anti-Jew sentiment could finally be stemmed.

Today, Britain, all Europe, along with the UN, has turned radically anti-Israel in their foreign policy position. Even the United States is wavering and cannot be counted on by Israel. What with the power of the Islamic states which make up nearly 1/3 of the world's populous, and the fact that these same states control most of the petroleum interest of the world, tiny Israel could be sacrificed on the altars of mammon. Except for the Evangelical Christian community, and God himself, Israel has no chance for survival. No peace treaty, which plays into the hands of those who intend Israel's destruction, can ever survive. Let's look at some of those treaties in the past and at the present.

THE PEACE TREATIES
OF PAST AND PRESENT

Historian Will Durant conjects that in 3400 years of

recorded human history, there has only been 268 years of peace. With such a statistic, if it were accurate, it is not probable that any peace initiative in such a volatile situation as the Middle East today could have a ghost of a chance to survive.

On September 13th, 1993, just 2300 days from the turn of the century, a celebrated agreement between PLO chairman Yasser Arafat and Prime Minister Yitzhak Rabin of Israel was signed in Washington in the presence of President Bill Clinton. Although great fanfare has been paid in the West, in actuality, it does not really deal with any significant area of the Middle East. However, it did start in motion some powerful international influences upon Israel.

I suppose that the saddest part of the Oslo agreement was that it once again brought into play a terrorist, which Israel at that time had paid a great price to get out of the picture. When Yasser Arafat had been run out of Jordan for his terrorist activities and his threat to the Crown of Jordan, he moved his terrorist organization into South Lebanon, where for years they terrorized and raped that country. The PLO destroyed Synagogues and Churches, massacred tens of thousands, and literally brought Southern Lebanon to devastation. From there Mr. Arafat reigned terror on Northern Israel.

Finally Israel, together with the Southern Lebanon Christian Army, led by Saad Hadad, removed Arafat and his cutthroats from Lebanon. During several days siege of downtown West Beirut, where Arafat and the PLO were cornered, Arafat sought refuge in any country that would allow him in, but none of the Muslim countries would allow him in. All knew him to be a dangerous revolutionary of the Marxist tradition. Finally Tunas allow him in where he was in exile until Bill Clinton resurrected him and forces him back on Israel.

In great detail the author can personally document the results in Southern Lebanon of Arafat's occupation there, for the author was personally invited to accompany the Israeli troops into Lebanon during the Campaign in 1982, and was a first hand observer of the onslaught on Arafat in Beirut on August 11. The truth about Arafat and Southern Lebanon has never yet been heard or told in any Western Media, even though every major Media outlet was there taking millions of feet of film and observing the same things the author saw. Of course, their sources for the reports they made to the American people came from the Red Crescent, run by Arafa's own brother.

Mr. Arafat comes from a long line of revolutionaries in the Middle East. His family came to Jerusalem only in recent times, after the Jews began to rebuild the Land. His cousin, Mufti Hag Amin al-Husseini, was a leader among the Arabs of East Jerusalem. The Mufti allied with Hitler during the Second World War, and was responsible for the deaths of many hundreds of Jews. In 1943, he personally was responsible for refusing an entrance into Palestine of 900 Jews who were fleeing from death camps in Romania. These people were turned over to the Nazis, eventually being executed in the gas chambers of Poland. As we have noted, it was also one of Arafat's brothers who ran the Red Crescent News Agency, a major PLO propaganda machine that fed most of the news reported by Western media. Yasser Arafat is directly responsible for the death of many thousands of women and children. He is a known murderer and rapist, and leads a band of cutthroat rebels who pillaged Jordan and Lebanon. No Middle East country would receive him until our own Bill Clinton forced him on Israel.

An acquaintance with other players in the Middle East may be helpful. Mr. Yitzhak Rabin, past Prime Minister of the State of Israel, and the main party in the Oslo peace initiative, was a Liberal Jew. He saw the answer to the problems of Israel as social and political and has little regard for the hope of a restored Temple Mount, city, or borders according to the old Biblical promises. He would have compromised anything for a political victory, including control of the Temple area, or land for peace regardless of the old promises. Many such Jews, being disillusioned by years of suffering like the Holocaust, believe the race should forget all their ancient dreams and cease to be a separate race.

Shamon Perez, negotiator for peace in Israel, is also a very liberal Jew. He served as vice President of the Socialist International, and is an avid student of Marx. He promised, if elected Prime Minister, to turn Jerusalem over to the Vatican. That's why Israel dumped him firmly in favor of Mr. Barak but Mr. Barak would have done worse. That's what put Mr. Ariel Sharon in power.

Ariel Sharon is an Orthodox Jew who believes in Bible promise and the restored State of Israel. However, as a dedicated Zionist, he is more inclined to rely on political strength than to trust in God. He is a strong Military leader, uncompromising on Israel's behalf. These qualities put him in good stead with the strong part of Israel, but puts him very much in the disfavor of the International Community.

The "Palestinians" that play such an important role, are mostly an invention of the anti-Israel press. Who these "Palestinians" are, and of what nationality they originate from, is much in question. There has never been a distinct people known as "Palestinians." What few people lived in the area known as Palestine prior to the Jewish State were a mixture of several peoples, including a small band of Jews who continued to live in Jerusalem and the surrounding land throughout the centuries.

The land has been for the most part desolate and uninhabited. For centuries after the Turks had taken control of the Holy Land in the 16th century and levied a tax against trees, the land had been rendered totally desolate. In "Holy Fields," Samuel Manning, who visited the Holy Land in 1874, wrote, "The Land is void and desolate without inhabitants."

Once the State of Israel began to prosper and bring in industry, jobs were created and tens of thousands of Muslims from over 29 different Islam states began to move in to enjoy jobs. Israel, as a free and Democratic Society, welcomed them. Many of those who now wish to destroy the State of Israel are those befriended by Israel.

The immortal Mark Twain also visited there in 1860, recorded in his book *Innocents Abroad*: "The hallowed spot....is untenanted by any living creature."

W. M. Thompson in his book *The Land and the Book* wrote in 1866: "How melancholy is this utter desolation! Not a house, not a trace of inhabitants, not even shepherds...."

It is recorded of the period that 99.9% of the land was totally desolate. A few Jews, Arabs, and other races inhabited small sections of Jerusalem. They were all known as the people of Palestine. I relate the foregoing simply to show that citizenship claims of an historical nature, made by the present population in Palestine, has little meaning. Most of the people claiming to be "Palestinian" must trace their birthplace to at least 29 different countries.

When the Jews began to return to the land in the early part of last century, they found it just as God had promised it would be after their disbursement from the land:

When you are scattered through the countries...I will...make the land ...more desolate than the wilderness...(Ezekiel 6:2,6,8,14).

In the first half of last century, as newly developing Jewish industry began to need labor, Arabs from surrounding countries began moving into Palestine. A sufficient number began to inhabit the land so that by 1948, when the State of Israel was created, the Arab populous, stirred up by a small band of revolutionaries like Yasser Arafat and his family, forsook their jobs and homes and fled unnecessarily. Trans-Jordan (as the country of Jordan was then known because it inhabited only the East side of the Jordan River) took East Jerusalem by military force along with all the mountainous parts of Israel. They killed or drove out all Jews and set up occupation of what became then known as the "West Bank" of Jordan. This gave the Arabs foothold in the land, who then began to claim citizenship of a country they called a "Palestinian State," a country that was non-existent at the time.

When the State of Israel, after being aggressed upon by five adjacent nations, won back the "West Bank" in 1967. They were marked as the aggressors, called "occupiers" and were set upon by the whole Arab world with the support of their lackey, the Western media. All of this in spite of the fact that the land known as the West Bank was mandated to Israel by both the League of Nations in 1922, and the United Nations, in 1948.

PRESENT PEACE A BOGUS PEACE

The foregoing is intended to give us a brief background of the situation so that hopefully, we may better understand the present peace process in light of Bible Prophecy.

As we understand it, the present Peace Treaties, past and present are a bogus peace, being forced upon Israel by the extortion of the U.S. State Department and the International Community of Nations (i.e. the World Government). More than 250,000 Jews have migrated from the former Soviet Union into tiny Israel. In order to absorb that many people, Israel needs the West Bank area, and great sums of money. The United States, in an act of what I would call plain blackmail and extortion, refused to co-sign a World Bank loan to Israel of $10 billion dollars, even though Israel is the only nation among our debtor nations that has never failed or defaulted on any loan. Israel was forced to enter into peace negotiations with Mister no-body Arafat, in order to secure the loan needed for the absorbing of so many people.

MULTI-NATIONAL TROOPS
TO ENFORCE THE PEACE

The Community of Nations, or UN, is forcing several other demands upon Israel. For instance, they are being forced to accept UN Resolution 242, 338 and other Resolutions, which are being used to pressure them to give up the West Bank and the Golan Heights. In order to enforce this "Peace," the Multi-national Forces, whose concept was formed by their first maneuvers in the Middle East at the Gulf War exercise, are beginning to gather around Israel, and that fact is very significant to Bible Prophecy.

The term, "Multi-national force," has become very familiar to us of recent times. We have witnessed the formation of the "World Government" in its political and economic form, but a world army was only suggested. Such international military organizations as NATO were conceived as the beginning of the idea. Bible prophecy teachers have been warning of the coming of a multi-national army for many years. Our own teaching has emerged from a consideration of the numerous texts, which mention a world army. The most prevalent identity of this world army in scriptures can be found in the term "armies of the nations." We have carefully considered virtually every reference to the term in its textual setting.

Forty-five times in the Prophets and in Revelation, the term Armies of the Nations, or its derivative, is used. All but six of those times, (39 times) it is used in direct relationship to the re-established State of Israel during the time of the Jews re-gathering. Almost all of the references have to do with involvement of the world's nations over problems relating to Jerusalem, and the Mountains of Israel (i.e. the West Bank). So we see extensive reference to the involvement of a Multi-national force in the affairs of the Middle East as they develop in the last days. According to present policy in the Middle East, the Multi-national forces are supposed to be there to assure the peace, both to Israel and the neighboring states. In fact, according to Bible Prophecy, they will bring down the final battle of the nations.

The intrigue increases, and the involvement of the World Order becomes even more fascinating when we focus on two other players in the scheme:

1. THE GREAT WORLD-WIDE, (International) CATHOLIC CHURCH

With its vast resources and power throughout the world on an international scale, and its rich holdings in Palestine, especially in Jerusalem, any movement on its part into the scenario of the area has great importance and must be noted. Its historical involvement with the 4th Beast of Daniel, the Roman Empire, and also the 7th head of the Beastly System, (i.e. the Holy Roman Empire) makes its movements into the Mid-East affairs even more significant.

On January 6th, 1994, in Jerusalem, the Vatican

signed an agreement with Israel, establishing an Embassy in Tel Aviv. The Pope himself visited soon after. Historically, the Church has refused to recognize the Jews, or the State of Israel, claiming that God's wrath fell on the Jews to destroy them for the Crucifixion of our Lord Jesus Christ. Therefore, according to them, any hate, persecution, or destruction of the Jews was fully justified in God's sight. The Jews were cut out of God's blessings and promises, and all of those promises were then conferred upon the Church. It was this conviction by the Church that incited the Inquisitions and the Crusades. Now the Catholic Church has forgiven the Jews. It is interesting how they seem to completely overlook Rome's own involvement in the Crucifixion.

In the agreement to establish diplomatic relations with Israel, the Vatican stated: "The Vatican is interested in attaining an international umbrella over Jerusalem."

It also stated: "Jerusalem is a delicate matter."

And further: "We need an International protocol to protect the peculiarity of Jerusalem (*Jeremiah Post*; Jan. 8,'94).

Here is the visible beginning of the end-time cooperation between Religious systems, and the Beastly World Empire systems working together to bring Antichrist's control over God's holy sights in Jerusalem.

2. KING JUAN CARLOS OF SPAIN

In November 1943, a momentous event took place; the import of such would not become evident to the world until our present time. It was accomplished in almost total secrecy. King Juan Carlos of Spain, the only actual ruling monarch in the world, met with Rabbi Getz at the Western Wall in Jerusalem. From there he visited the Knesset where he met all the dignitaries of the State of Israel. It has been over 500 years, (since the Inquisitions in fact) that either the State of Spain or the Jews would have anything to do with each other.

Let us remember that it was at the invitation of King Juan Carlos of Spain that the peace negotiations between the PLO and the State of Israel were held in Madrid, Spain. To those who understand the prophetic implications of these facts, all of this is of prime importance. When we realize that deeply hidden in a secret and esoterical order of the kingly families of Europe, there is a title held by certain Kings-in-Waiting, known as the "KING OF JERUSALEM." This title has been in existence ever since the first of eight Crusades, the first organized by Godfrey de Bouillon of Lorraine. A German alliance with several other kings backed an effort to reclaim Jerusalem from the Muslims. The alliance stormed Palestine, took Jerusalem, and on July 15, 1099, placed Bouillon's brother, Baldwin, on a throne and crowned him King of Jerusalem. The control over Jerusalem did not last long, and Baldwin's throne was soon overturned. The hope of putting a European king on the throne in Jerusalem has inspired a secret order within the families of the Kings of Europe ever since. Within that secret order is a system of "kings" who still dream of ruling a world Empire, and who keep alive the ancient hope that one of them would become the long hoped for "Messiah" King of prophecy. In fact, such a move would but fulfill the abomination spoken of in

Daniel, Matthew 24:15 and II Thessalonians 2:4.

All of this becomes highly significant when we realize that King Juan Carlos today holds the title "KING OF JERUSALEM." He holds heir to the title on the Bourbon side of the Royal families of Europe. On the Habsburg side, Otto Von Habsburg, son of the last reigning king of the old Holy Roman Empire, holds the title, whose throne was brought down by the crusades of Napoleon and finally by the first world war. There is some competition between the families of the Kings for this coveted position. To our study, it is of great significance that plans are made to put a European King in Jerusalem in the future, an event that would perfectly harmonize with specific predictions of prophecy. Juan Carlos, King of Jerusalem, coming to Jerusalem, establishing diplomatic relationship with the Jews, and hosting the peace initiative in his own capital city of Madrid, Spain, certainly adds prophetic significance to these events.

Dr. Taylor, of TODAY IN BIBLE PROPHECY's radio broadcast, has written a book entitled *Antichrist King* in which he has shown strong evidence for Juan Carlos as the final Beastly King. Whether or not this is so, we do know that powerful forces are working today to that very end, and that an ominous World Government will internationalize Jerusalem and eventually bring a strong man into control there.

Henry Kissinger was the first to suggest the internationalizing of Jerusalem. He made such an impact toward World Order and the emergence of a world strong man, that the editor of *TIME* Magazine, wrote in an editorial on July 1, '74:

> Kissinger's achievements have, at long last, justi-
> fied the establishment of a new political office
> which I sincerely hope the United States will con-
> sider---Enter, Mr. President Planet Earth.

We see here the Great Beastly Empire, the 8th to come out of the 7th, (i.e. the World Order) joining with the Mother of Harlots, to put a European King on a throne in Jerusalem, with title King of Jerusalem. This will force Israel to compromise her Biblical position, divide her land, and accept a bogus peace with a non-existent state, (i.e. the "Palestinians") and to declare Jerusalem, not in capitol of Israel, but World Property.

In perfect keeping with Bible prophecy, under administration of the Beastly World Government, and in harmony with the Harlot, Jerusalem will be placed in the care of a strong man, who will "confirm a covenant" with the Jews for a period of 7 years (Daniel 9:27). To enforce the peace and the covenant, the "Armies of the Nations," or the Multi-national forces of our day, will encircle Jerusalem. The internationalizing of Jerusalem and the division of the land, together with the interference of the World Order in the affairs of Jerusalem and the Holy Mount runs contrary to God's plan for the area.

MAN'S PLANS AND GOD'S PROMISES

Oslo was man's plans and not God's. It was a miserable failure. Camp David and Wye, under Bill Clinton was the work of a man more interested in his legacy than Israel's interest or God's plan. Mr. Clinton was totally embarrassed when, after forcing Mr. Barak to concede more than he or Israel could allow, Mr. Arafat turned down the best opportunity for a Palestinian State, and set off years of Intafada. Mr. Bush, to appease the Arab States for their support in the Coalition against Iraq, has initiated what he calls "The Road Map," but it has also failed.

The Peace Treaties initiated and promoted by the International Community, all propose to negotiate plans for Jerusalem. However it has not been God's time or plan. Several dates have been set for the "final solution," and the hope of settling the Jerusalem question. Powerful elements in Israel and among the Evangelical churches of the world will not bow to World Government control over Jerusalem because it is not in God's Plan. The wrath of the World Police Force will come down on the churches world-wide, as well as on Israel. Armageddon is just around the corner, beloved. Jeremiah 25:31, comes to mind:

> *A noise shall come even to the ends of the earth; for the Lord hath a controversy with the nations, he will plead with all flesh; he will give them that are wicked to the sword, saith the Lord.*

God's controversy with the World Order of nations seems to be their interference in the affairs of Jerusalem, as we will discuss in detail later. He is also very concerned with the division of the land, as the following scriptures will demonstrate.

> *Behold, in those days, and in that time, when I shall bring again the captivity of Judah and Jerusalem (the Jews return), I will also gather all nations, and will bring them down into the Valley of Jehoshaphat, and will plead with them there for my people and for my heritage Israel, whom they have scattered among the nations and PART-ED MY LAND (Joel 3:1,2).*

> *Thus saith the Lord; For three transgressions of the children of Amman, (i.e. Jordan) and for four, I will not turn away the punishment thereof (Amos 1:13).*

And what is the problem? "That they might enlarge their border."

This is precisely what Jordan did when she took the West Bank, or the Mountains of Israel. She enlarged her borders and tried to make two parts to her nation. How well this fits the words of prophecy in Ezekiel 35:10. Speaking of Mt. Seir, which is a scriptural term for Edom, (now designated Jordan) and in relationship to possessing the Mountains of Israel (i.e. the West Bank) we find these words:

"Because thou, (Jordan) has said, These two nations and these two countries shall be mine, and we will possess it, whereas the Lord was there." The Lord goes on to pronounce judgment. "I will do according to thine anger —I will make myself known among them when I have judged thee —I have heard all thy blasphemies which thou hast spoken against the Mountains of Israel, saying, they are laid desolate, they are given us to consume."

But, we must ask, who gave the Mountains of Israel to Jordan? Rather, they simply possessed it by war and are trying to lay claim to it by inheritance. The World Community of nations is willing to give it to them by UN resolution. Such a controversy has ensued between Israel and Jordan that even they have backed out and left the issue hanging for years (since 1967). Jordan tried to "consume" the West Bank by incorporating it into its own land. This only brought her into conflict with God and his plan for the area, not to mention the conflict with Israel. The Judgment of God has rested on Jordan ever since. Jeremiah 31: 17 states clearly God's plan for the area, "...*and there is hope in thine end,* (Israel), *saith the Lord, that thy children shall come again to their own border.*" God has no other intention or plan than to eventually turn the West Bank over to the State of Israel.

Jeremiah 1:12 says that God is watching over His word to fulfill it. We may be absolutely sure that God's purpose will eventually be accomplished, even at the expense of every nation on earth. God's Word also promises eternal life to those who put their trust in Jesus Christ as Lord and Savior. As we see His faithfulness in keeping His Word to Israel, how it encourages us that He will also keep His Word to us.

There is another scenario working in correlation to the foregoing stated events. It is concerning JORDAN AND THE WEST BANK. Let us proceed now to examine it and it's meaning to us as relates to Bible prophecy.

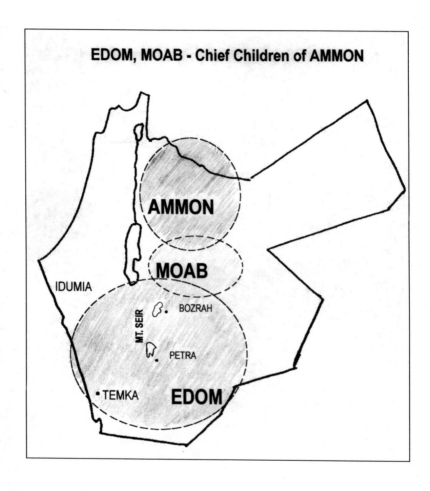

CHAPTER 2

JORDAN AND THE WEST BANK

WHY THIS PEACE WILL LAST

Let us be reminded of the statement made by Joseph de Coursey Jr., editor of INTELLIGENCE DIGEST. It is not always good to be repetitive, but because the declaration is, we think, such an important allegation by such an important and influential person, it bears worthiness of repetition:

"I've come to the conclusion that what is happening in the Middle East is going to bring the world to its last battle. I know nothing about the Bible I draw this conclusion from data we gather for the Digest."

Let us carefully note this part of the statement: "What is happening in the Middle East is going to bring the world to its last battle."

We have said that Israel is God's time clock. Nowhere is this so evident as it is in events involving what is known today as the West Bank. Today, it is the issue of the "Territories," as they are called, that has the world on alert. The West Bank, or in Biblical terms, the Mountains of Israel, or Judea and Samaria, has become the defining event of our time. No issue has caught the world's attention like the Palestinian issue and the resulting terrorism in Israel since WWII. The longer it goes, the more diplomats try to solve the problem, no matter whether it be the United States, UN, EU, Russia, or the Muslim States such as Egypt, or Saudi Arabia, the situation only gets worse.

The crisis would not be so difficult if it were not for two factors, which interplay in the picture. One is the involvement of Marxist type revolutionary tactics and propaganda that has been so successful in disrupting peace in many nations during the cold war. Such tactics have been defeated in most areas, but is still playing a major roll in the volatile Middle East. It will continue to disrupt all possibility of peace as long as Yasser Arafat is in control, for like Castro in Cuba, he is a hard core revolutionary who does not intend peace, but overthrow. The second factor is a 4000-year-old hate, perpetuated, (that is taught and propagated), among the Arab and Muslim people. We will discuss this hate in detail later.

THE PARADOX OF JORDAN

Although Jordan has become aware of its error in taking

the West Bank during the '48 war, and has tried to back out of the issue; it must be remembered that it was in fact, Jordan, whose actions started this whole debacle in the first place. It will be interesting to watch the future developments of this crisis, and Jordan's involvement. Concerning Jordan of the last days, there is a fascinating paradox in the Scriptures. In Ezekiel 35, God promises Judgment on Mount Seir. Seir is in south Jordan (see page 20). Jordan will be punished severally for her role in shedding *"the blood of the children of Israel."* (Ezekiel 35:5) and appointing *"my land into their possession,"* (Ezekiel 36:5) Still there is a prophetic promise that in some sense Jordan will be spared from the Antichrist, (Daniel 11:41) and will protect the fleeing Jews from the West Bank, or Judea, (Matthew 24:15, and Isaiah 16:1-4 together with Revelation 12:14-17, etc.) This protection by God, and involving at least the territory of Jordan, if not the State itself, will be for 3 1/2 years during the reign of the Antichrist.

We must also remember that Jordan has been given control over the coveted Temple Mount, which rancors both the Palestinians and the Jews alike. It is then a point well taken that no peace negotiations can be seriously attempted without the involvement of Jordan. It remains to be seen how Jordan will react and how strong her commitment is, to have peace with Israel until the final solution.

Prophecies concerning the West Bank and Jordan can readily be found. By examining them closely, we find more of those fantastic prophecies.   For instance, there are specific promises made to Israel concerning borders that were promised to her during the days of her return back to the land.   These exact borders become a great matter of controversy, as we have shown in the previous chapter, not only between peoples, but also between God and the people of the land.   An examination of the background and history of the Covenant, which God made concerning the land, will help us understand.

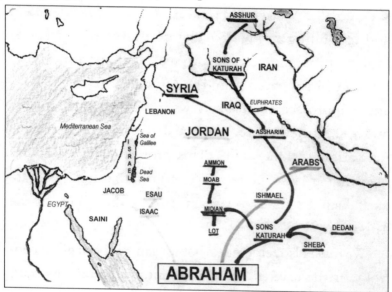

THE COVENANT AND THE LAND IN OLD TESTAMENT TEXTS

First, we would like to clarify what we think to be a very great error. Teachings during the early era of Christianity, and too often carried over in doctrine today, taught that God had given up on the Jews, destroyed their race, and transferred all the promises to the Church.

This gross error has inspired two very serious heresies in our world, both past and present, and has been responsible for most of the persecution toward the Jews, and much of the confusion in Eschatological teaching and prophetic blunder today. The first can be identified as the Anglo-Israel idea, which tries to make the Anglo-Saxons, and thus the Americans, the 10 lost tribes of Israel. This is a principal error. However, similar ideas have been accepted and taught in many of the mainline churches and even in some Evangelical churches today.

The second very serious inaccuracy has been around since the Catholic Church developed its Universal status and decided that it was God's total authority on Earth, and the Pope was the Vicar of Christ. To justify the Crusades, the Inquisitions, etc, they instituted an interpretation of the Old Testament, which became known as "Replacement Theology." It's premises was simply this: The Jews have been forsaken for their crucifixion of Christ, God has given up on them. They no longer have a place in history, and all of the promises made to them by God in the Old Testament are now transferred to the Church. The Reformation leaders sadly picked up this theme and taught it widely, making it a part of the Doctrine of the early Reformation Churches. Consequently it as been adopted by many mainline churches today. To our collective shame, some Evangelical Churches and individual preachers have also adopted it as well.

In many ways, the Church has been disposed to ignore the direct and clear contextual setting of many Old Testament promises, by interpreting Israel as the Church. Thus we have often claimed the promises which rightfully belonged to a restored Israel. We may find clear evidence of this when we observe most of the chapter headings and marginal comments in most modern Bibles today. Let us remember those comments and headings are not part of the inspired text. They certainly come from respectable commentators, and for inspirational and hermeneutical purposes may be used in the context of the Church, since we can certainly believe correctly that all scripture is given for our admonition upon whom the end of the world falls (I Corinthians 10:11). It is also true that every scripture is inspired and profitable to us, the Church (II Timothy 3:16). However, most of the time it will be advantageous for the serious student of the Scriptures to ignore the comments and read the text within the context for exactly what it says and means.

Nowhere can we support such theories as Anglo-Israel and Replacement Theology. Those who did not expect the Jews to remain a separate people until the end of time, would be very oppressed today to find them everywhere in all nations of the world. Their race still exists in spite of the Crusades, Pogroms, Inquisitions, and the Holocaust. Those who did not expect the Jews to return to the Holy Land and become a nation among the nations in the end have certainly been proven wrong in their interpretation of Scripture.

By reading the prophecies and promises within their actual text and context, both in Old and New Testaments, we will find that God never intended that the seed of Abraham to vanish forever. He promises a remnant would survive and return to the land. When we leave these promises in that context we discover some very exciting and revealing prophecies which no doubt speak to us clearly of today's events.

None of the promises of God to Abraham, as concerning the land, the city of Jerusalem, or the Temple Mount, belong to the Church. If it were so, then I submit that God could have blessed the Crusades in their efforts to make Christendom owners of the land of Israel. It must be clearly understood that God has made no promise of an earthly city to the Church, He has promised only a Heavenly one to come. Paul clearly stated that fact, while Jerusalem was a great consideration in his day and while Rome was supreme. It is made plain to us that "We have here no continuing city," but we have one to come. With Abraham, we look for a City whose builder and maker is God. We are *come to the city of the living God.* And it is clearly stated in scripture *"God hath prepared for them that city"* (Hebrews 13:14, Hebrews 12:22, and Hebrews ll:16 respectively). Our citizenship is in Heaven;

Our City is the New Jerusalem coming down from Heaven. Our hope is in Heaven from whence we look for our Lord Jesus Christ to come and take us there.

The Jews have a different promise, which involves an earthly guarantee. They are promised a country, a city, and a Temple. And the Jewish people, contrary to the expectation of those earlier Christians, have kept their identity throughout the long ages. Specific promises are made to them relating to the restoration of the land of Israel, the return of the people to that land, and the rebuilding of the city of Jerusalem and the Temple. The entire motif of the Old Testament is centered in that promise and expectation, together with its ultimate fulfillment in a coming "Messiah" who would eventually redeem the Jewish people, while at the same time take out of the Gentiles a people for his name sake (Acts 1514-17 and Romans 11: 25,26). Ezekiel 37:25 is an example of such a promise:

And they shall dwell in the land that I have given unto Jacob my servant, wherein your fathers have dwelt; and they shall dwell therein, even they and their children, and their children's children forever. And David my servant will be their prince forever.

These promises, and over 200 other texts cannot be interpreted as belonging to the Babylonish return in the days of Ezra and Nehamiah, but must be seen in the greater context of fulfillment in the last days. Certainly for instance, David did not return to his throne in the Babylonish Return.

Over 4000 years ago, (1000 years before David claimed Jerusalem as the Capitol of Israel, and nearly 500 years before the Exodus from Egypt) a young Iraqi boy by the name of Abraham, heard God's call. Abraham was to separate from his pagan father and the idolatrous society in Mesopotamia, which had so soon developed shortly after the flood of Noah. In fact, Noah's son Shem was probably still alive when Abraham left. Abraham's goal was a country that he would afterwards receive as an inheritance (Genesis 12). It was right after the Tower of Babel dispersion, when many worldly-minded people so hated God for the flood and for the inference in their "World Order" and "humanitarian" efforts at the Tower of Babel. This was also in the days of Nimrod's earlier Kingdoms, and during the time of his rebellion against God and the development of his deeply corrupt heresies. Abraham's father and possibly some of the family had gotten caught up in some of those perversions.

The Lord God made Abraham a certain promise at that time:

And the Lord said unto Abram, ..Lift up now, thine eyes, and look from the place where thou art northward, and southward, and eastward, and westward, for all the land which thou seest, to thee will I give it and to thy seed for ever

(Genesis 13:4-15).

Abraham was standing at that moment at the high place of Bethel, in what is now known as the West Bank of Jordan. Do you see the seriousness of separating the West Bank from the Promise of God to Abraham, and making it a separate State from Israel?

If we were to leave out of Israel's borders the area known as the West Bank, we would eliminate from God's promise to Abraham, not only the very spot where he was standing, but all the land northward, southward and eastward. Therefore, we would leave out of the promise such cities as:

Shilo, where the ark rested before the Temple was built.

Bethel, where Jacob saw heaven.

Hebron, David's first throne, and burial place of Abraham, Sarah and others.

Judea, and all the Mountains of Israel.

Bethlehem, where Jesus was born.

Jerusalem, where the Temple stood -- Selah!

This covenant was confirmed to Abram by God in Chapter 12, and repeated again in Chapter 15, where the borders were set. From the Euphrates River in Iraq, to the River of Egypt, the Nile was promised to all of Abram's seed. That very land has been possessed by the sons of Abram ever since, for we must remember that the Arabs are also the sons of Abraham, as are the Edomites. If this fact was made clear and accepted by both the Jews and Arabs, instead of Israel implying that their border should extend to the Nile and Euphrates, it would simplify things in the Middle East. While it is this author's opinion that the Millenial Israel will possess what is known today as "Greater Israel," (from the Nile to the Euphrates), we believe the present State was only promised what Abraham could see from Bethel and what was included in Jacob's possession, namely the land of Canaan (see Ezekiel 37:25).

While all of the Middle East was promised to all of Abram's sons, the land which was shown to Abraham from his position at Bethel, that little bridge of land on the Mediterranean coast and extending Eastward to the Jordan River was promised to Isaac alone. Isaac was Abram's miracle son. Genesis 17:7,8, while speaking of an "everlasting covenant," gives this promise:

> *I will give unto thee, and to thy seed after thee, the land wherein thou art a stranger, all the land of Canaan, for an everlasting possession.*

In verse 21 the Lord makes the covenant promise specifically to Isaac, who had not yet been born.

> *But my covenant will I establish with Isaac...*

The same promise was reaffirmed unto Jacob,

whose name was changed to "Israel." Therefore the promise is extended to the twelve sons and their tribes, who are better known as the twelve tribes of Israel. The motivation to keep themselves a separated race and return to the land is found in verse 9:

> And God said unto Abraham, Thou shalt keep my covenant therefore, thou, and thy seed after thee in their generations.

We see it as an obligation pressed upon the Jewish people by God himself, inspired of international community interference, to forever possess the Land of Promise in the latter days of the return.

According to Leviticus 25:23-24, the land was never to be sold, nor was foreign possession ever to be allowed. It was forever to remain the heritage of Abraham's seed through Isaac and Jacob.

> The land shall not be sold forever, for the land is mine. For you are strangers and sojourners with me. And in all the land of your possession ye shall grant a right of redemption for the land.

God blessed Ishmael also, the father of the Arabs, and gave them all the rest of the land of the Middle East. However Scripture foresees he would be a wild race, with his hand against every man, and because of his wildness, every man's hand would be against him. This has always been an accurate assessment of the spirit of the Arabian people (See Genesis 16: 10-12).

While the Bible is full of references to this promise and the covenant between God, Abraham and his posterity, especially as it concerns the city of Jerusalem, the Temple Mount and the Promised Land, the Koran has no mention of Jerusalem whatsoever. However the Koran does agree that the City and Land must belong to the Jews in the latter time. To the Muslim people we must say, if you will read and obey your own holy writ, it will tell you the same as the Bible concerning the promise of land to Isaac. For instance, Sura 5, "The Table," describes the land reserved for the Jews, and also blesses the Jews in the land and forecasts their return to the land. It also says that all of this will happen in the end of days. More reference to this subject can be found in chapter 4.

GENTILE OCCUPATION

In the Book of Deuteronomy chapters 30 and 31, God promises to bless the Jewish people in their land. However, he also pronounced a curse upon them if they failed to obey his laws and commandments, for which they were to be disbursed from the land into all nations. From there they would return to the land in the last days.

Accordingly, because of their disobedience, the Babylonian King Nebuchadnezzar, was allowed to come into Israel, sack Jerusalem, destroy the Temple, and possess the land. In order to break the power of the Jews in the land; Nebuchadnezzar carried captive all influential Jews out of the land and into Babylon. Assyria, before Babylon, had already defeated and occupied the northern 10 tribes of Israel. Babylon was the first of four great kingdoms which Daniel saw occupying in succession the land of Israel. In all, seven great Empires would possess and occupy the land before the final days. The seven heads in the Beast of Revelation represented these seven.

During these occupations, which lasted from 586 BC to the present, the Jews were allowed to live in the land for the most part, but were only counted as a province of the ruling power. Even today the occupiers of the land are foreigners. The *Jerusalem Post* for July 11, '94, p 6 records:

> "Present Palestinians are Syrian Colonists sent by Rome to defeat Bar Kochba (132 AD). Rome changed the name from 'Judea,' to 'Palestine', kicked out the Jews..."

The Jews were then dispersed into the entire world and the land of Israel totally occupied by foreigners until now.

Throughout time since 586 BC, the land has been occupied by Assyrians, Babylonians, Persians, Greeks, Romans, Byzantines, the Muslims, Crusaders, and Turkish Ottomans. Finally, until 1948, the Allied Forces of Europe and the Western Alliances occupied it.

THE BIRTH OF THE MODERN
STATE OF ISRAEL

WWI saw the fall of the Ottoman Turks, who had joined Germany. General Allenby, of the British Army, was sent to what is now Cairo, with orders to deliver Jerusalem from Turk control. Allenby, a very pious and religious man with great respect of the Holy Places of Jerusalem, sent a telegram to King George of England and asked how he might drive the Turks out of the city without doing damage to the Holy Places. The King responded in a telegram that read: "Make it a matter of prayer." Allenby retired to his quarters after giving orders that he was not to be disturbed, and after a night of earnest prayer, felt the Lord was going to help him deliver the city without destruction.

Allenby moved his troops to the Jordan Plains, just across from Jericho, built a bridge across the Jordan River, a bridge named after him and in existence today, and prepared to march up to Jerusalem.

At his disposal were six small aircraft of the old WWI type, with open cockpit, and double wings. Allenby sent those crafts in reconnaissance over Jerusalem to locate the Turk positions and to drop pamphlets in Arabic warning the people of his intent to take Jerusalem. By this time Allenby had moved his troops to a spot still identified today just north of the Old City of Jerusalem.

The Turks, never having actually seen a plane, did not

know what they were and thought they might be from Heaven. To add to their superstitious notions, the name "Allenby" pronounced in Arabic sounded like "Allah-bay," (Alla-neba) which means "Servant of the Lord." The "servant of the Lord is coming," was what it sounded like to the Turks who spoke Arabic. As they read the pamphlets dropped from the sky, they interpreted the information to mean that the servant of Allah was coming and demanding that they lay down arms. When the little noisy planes came buzzing down over the housetops of Jerusalem, it so frightened the Turks that they abandoned their positions and fled from Jerusalem, totally vacating the city. General Allenby and his troops were completely unknowledgeable of the retreat of the Turks.

The next morning, the Army was in preparation to enter the city. Early in the morning the cook, an Irishman, found he was in need of eggs. Hearing roosters crowing, he said to himself, "Where there are roosters, there are eggs." So he proceeded toward Jerusalem to find some eggs. Suddenly, he was met by a delegation out of Jerusalem that included the Mayor and many of the city officials. To his surprise, they handed him the Keys to the City of Jerusalem. He argued with them that he only came for eggs, they would have to see General Allenby for their business. Eventually Allenby was called, and to his great delight, the city surrendered with only a little bit of fire.

God had answered Allenby's prayer in a most marvelous way, but more than that, and of greater interest to us, he had also fulfilled in detail a most fascinating verse of prophecy. Isaiah the prophet, while fore-viewing the events of the last day surrounding Israel's return to the land and the eventual deliverance of Jerusalem from Gentile occupation, saw a fascinating scene that very closely parallels the events just described. In Isaiah, chapter 31 and verse 5 we read:

> As *birds flying* (airplanes), *so will the Lord of hosts defend Jerusalem; defending also he will deliver it; and passing over he will preserve it.*

At that time, with England firmly in control of the Holy Land, the Allies of WWI gave her mandate over the land. A strong move to declare Palestine a homeland for the Jews began to come to the forefront, led by Theodore Herzl, father of modern political Zionism. In convening a Jewish congress in 1897, Herzl declared:

> "The object of Zionism is to establish for the Jewish people a publicly and legally assured home in Palestine."

When the war ended, after "carnage, blockade, and starvation" (Am. Encyclopedia), and with "Pogroms, executions, and wholesale deportations" (Ibid.) it seemed impossible to sustain Jewish corporate life in Europe.

The Balfour Declaration of 1917, however, held forth for the Jewish people a new glowing vision and hope of a homeland in Palestine. Five years later, the newly established League of Nations confirmed the declaration and mandated all of Palestine as a homeland for the Jews. Alas, this did not seem to settle the Jewish problem in Europe. It took WWII and the Holocaust to bring world attention to the needs of the Jewish people. By this time the League of Nations no longer existed, and the new United Nations, with its headquarters in New York City, had taken its place. On November 29, 1947 after three world-rocking days of debate, it seemed the whole world stood against the mandate designating Palestine as a homeland for the Jews. Suddenly, the Soviet Union took an unexpected turn, and in an action that could not be easily explained, joined the United States in recommending Palestine as a home for the Jews.

On that memorable day, May 15, 1948, the State of Israel was born. For the first time in over 25 centuries, the Flag of David was raised over the Holy Land. The Jews had their homeland again. It is of singular interest to note that that very date was the day that had been set aside by the Jews for nearly 2000 years as the day they celebrated the Promise of Return. The budding of the fig tree was the symbol of that celebration. The budding of the fig tree represented the budding of the new State of Israel. With that in mind let us refer to Jesus' words in

Matthew 24:32, 33:

> *Now learn a parable of the fig tree; When his branch is yet*
> *tender, and putteth forth leaves, ye know that summer is*
> *nigh: So likewise ye, when ye shall see all these things,*
> *know that it is near, even at the door.*

I believe, and our belief can be adequately established by supporting scriptures that, in His perfect foreknowledge, the Lord was referring to the celebration of
the budding of the fig tree as a symbol of the birth of
Israel.

Peace was short-lived for the new state of Israel.
Immediately, seven Arab States refused to honor the UN
mandate, and declared war upon the newly formed State.
Israel, by miracles and sheer courage, defended itself well and
won the war, thus establishing herself among the nations.

JORDAN TOOK MOUNTAINS OF ISRAEL

There was a serious loss, however. The "Palestinian"
nation, then known as Transjordan in-as-much as its
border was across the Jordan River to the East, pressed
across the Jordan River, took most all of the mountainous parts of the Holy Land, including all of the old city
of Jerusalem with it's Temple Mount. Transjordan then
changed its name to JORDAN, claiming property on
both sides of the Jordan River. They divided the country into two parts; one called the West Bank of Jordan,

the other Jordan proper. By annexing the newly called West Bank, they now controlled all of the ancient Holy Places including the Temple Mount. They kicked all of the Jews out, forcing them into massive refugee camps. They destroyed many of the Synagogues and Jewish places of worship. It is strange how you never hear anything about these refugees. One reason is the sheer bias of Western news sources. The other is that Israel did not leave them in refugee camps for international propaganda pawns, as did Jordan, Lebanon and Syria, but quickly found places for them in the Israeli work force. Contrary to both Bible promises to the Jews, and Koran teaching, the Palestinian State of Transjordan committed both Biblical and international transgression.

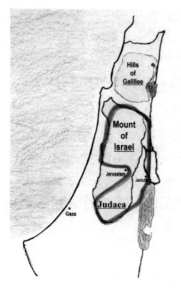

Jordan occupied the "West Bank" until 1967. On June 6th of that year, once again all the neighboring states around Israel declared war on Israel with the intent to destroy her. In six glorious days Israel not only took all of the Sinai, the Golan Heights and Gaza, but took back the West Bank from Jordan, including the city of Jerusalem and the

Temple Mount. (Refer to illustration.)

For 2000 years Jews around the world (when ending one of their celebrations) would go outside, face toward Jerusalem, and cry out their greatest hope:

"Next year, Jerusalem."

When the Israeli solders reached the Western Wall of the Temple Mount, they dropped their weapons, and ran to the Wall to pray and worship. They were at last realizing an ancient dream. In 1982 Israel declared Jerusalem as its capitol forever, and moved the center of its government to Western Jerusalem. However, problems were just beginning for them. The UN immediately revolted and demanded that Israel "give back" the West Bank to Jordan even though it was Jordan who had "occupied" the land, not Israel. Control of the Temple Mount was given back to Jordan, and terrorism reigned in the area. The Arabs, calling themselves "Palestinians" began to lay claim to Jerusalem and the West Bank. Israel has suffered in continual siege ever since.

All of this is very important in consideration of Bible Prophecy, which we hope to explore with you in the next few pages.

In occupying the West Bank and commanding control of the Temple Mount, the Hassumite kingdom of Jordan and its King stepped out of the shadows of obscurity and into the lime light of prophecy. By laying claim to the Mountains of Israel (i.e. the West Bank), and taking authority over the Temple Mount, God and His Word has been challenged, and His anger is soon to be known. All of this has set the stage for the final battle of the nations, but also for the great day of God's final manifestation and glory.

WEST BANK IS THE MOUNTAINS OF ISRAEL

First of all let us identify the West Bank in prophecy and show why we have been calling it the Mountains of Israel and Judea and Samaria. If you study the geological map of the Holy Land, which shows the mountainous part of the area, and draw a circle around the mountainous portion, you will be startled to find that your outline of the mountains of the area almost exactly match the lines of the territories known as the West Bank. It becomes evident then, that the West Bank is in fact what the Bible speaks of as the Mountains of Israel.

A quick search of scripture will reveal this to be so, and when we identify the prophetic scriptures that deal with the Mountains of Israel, we discover some very interesting texts, which must be applied to the West Bank of our day. For instance, we find what might be called a blow by blow description of the very things that are presently taking place in the Holy Land today, as relates to the West Bank. An example can be found in chapters

34-37 of the book of Ezekiel, where the Mountains of Israel are the specific subject of that prophecy. Let us examine those chapters more carefully.

We will note first of all, that Mount Seir is the problem (v.2,3). Mount Seir is in the lower central part of Jordan, and was a term identifying the people of the area now known as Jordan. It is Mount Seir's (or Jordan's) involvement with the Mountains of Israel (i.e. the West Bank), that is the subject of God's harsh judgment upon them. Let's look at some very interesting parallels in these prophecies to the events surrounding the West Bank, or the Mountains of Israel today.

In chapter 34, verse 29, there is a specific prophecy. It is during a time when Mount Seir is laying claim to the Mountains of Israel, and God is promising special blessing. In siege, when the people are starving in Jerusalem, God promises to send a special plant; A "plant of renown." It was during Jordan's siege of Jerusalem in 1948, that starvation was being forced upon the Jews. Suddenly, a new weed began to grow all over the Jewish sector. It was a spinach-like plant. Just as the British left, forsaking Jerusalem to the Muslim hoard, three days of rain fell unseasonably and the "Khubeeza plant" sprang up everywhere. In the book *"Oh Jerusalem,"* this incident is recorded. The Jewish women are said to have begun singing and dancing, and saying:

"When He brought us out of Egypt it was the manna.

Now He has sent rain for the cisterns, and Khubeeza.."

Verse 5 of the 35th chapter speaks of a "perpetual hatred" found in the people of Jordan toward the people of Israel. Literally, an "ancient hate" (Ezekiel 25:15- that "old hate," or "ancient hostility") is suggested. Perpetuated hate is a hate which is propagated by teaching, purposefully encouraged by those who intentionally, and for their own benefit, continue to perpetuate it.

Certainly we can find that very hate represented in actions against the Jews in Israel today. Much of that hate is generated because of the Mountains of Israel. Most of the terror and animosity in the Middle East can be directly related to the West Bank Territories, and Jordan (Mt. Seir) is the focal point, for it was Jordan's hate of Israel that created the West Bank in the first place. Following are some quotations from the Ministry of Education in Jordan, which can be found quoted in the book "The Mountains of Israel" by Norma Archbold, (A Phoebe's Song Publication). Each of these quotations demonstrates the extreme hate perpetuated by Jordan:

From a 1966 3rd year Jr. High book, *"Modern World History"*:

> "The Jews in Europe were persecuted and despised because of their corruption, meanness, and treachery."

From a 1964 1st Year High School book, "Glances at Arab Society" p 117:

"Israel was born to die."

From a 1963 edition of "Religious Ordinances Reader":

"The Jews--exiled and despised since by nature they are vile, greedy and enemies of all mankind."

Found in a 1963 5th year elementary study, "Basic Syntax and Spelling":

"We shall expel all the Jews."

For example, analyze the following sentence:

"We shall expel all Jews from Arab Countries."

The book *"Zionist Imperialism"* p.249 teaches the ninth grade students:

"Israel shall not live if the Arabs stand fast in their hatred."

"People all over the world have come to realize that Hitler was right-would that he had finished the job."

These quotations are only a small sample of preponderance of evidence to show the perpetuated hate being propagated against the Jews in the whole of the Arab world today, and especially in the West Bank. From these few quotations drawn from the school systems of Jordan we can quickly see an evident fulfillment of verse 5.

We are told that the Palestinian Authorities indoctrinate hate into children at Day Camps. A recent release from the B'nai B'rith International revealed a study of 68 Syrian school texts spanning grades 1-12. The study quoted scores of statements from the school texts which taught children to hate Jews and Israel with a passion. This is especially disturbing when we realize that Syria chairs the UN Security Council and Co-chairs the UN Human Rights Commission which are headquartered in Geneva.

We may find also from other sources, the same perpetuated hate. Especially is this hate propagated in the religious communities of the Muslims. For example, Palestinian television broadcasts regular calls from the Moslem Clerics to hate and destroy the Jew. From the Mosque in Gaza, a Moslem minister, Zayed bin Sultan Aal Nahyan, said:

"The Jews are Jews, whether Labor or Likud.... They do not have any moderates or any advocates of peace. They are all liars....O brother believers, the criminals, the terrorists are the Jews, who have butchered our children, orphaned them, widowed our women and desecrated our holy places...They are the terrorists. They are the ones who must be butchered and killed, as Allah the Almighty said: fight them: Allah will torture them at your hands, and will humiliate them and will help you to overcome them, and will relieve the minds of the believers."

And then he said that the dowry of paradise was to:

"Fight in the path of Allah, and kill and be killed. Allah has purchased from the believers their persons and their property in return for the promise that they shall have paradise, for they fight in the cause of Allah, and they slay the enemy and are slain. The Jews are the allies of the Christians......all of them are in agreement against monotheists...."There is no God but Allah and Muhammad is his messenger. They, (Jews and Christians) are against you O Muslims.... Have no mercy on the Jews, no matter where they are ...Fight them. Wherever you are, kill those Jews and those Americans who are like them."

One Palestinian woman interviewed again on PA Television said:

"All we ask is that the Arab countries stand by our side, give us weapons, and we, on our own, will... kill them; slaughter them, all of them. All we ask is weapons and we won't spare a single Jew."

Again in Ezekiel 35 verse 5 we will find another interesting statement. It is said that Jordan had:

"Shed the Blood of the children of Israel by the force of the sword in the time of their calamity."

The above was to be at the time that God had forgiven the Jews iniquity and brought judgment upon Israel to an end. Of course, this important statement places this prophecy during the time of the people's return to the Land.

I need not comment long on the shed blood of Israel that was let during the War of Independence, and Jordan certainly had its share of blame. The first 900 Jews to escape Romania tried to come into Palestine to avoid the German Extermination camps. None other than Arafat's own cousin refused them entrance into the land. They eventually ended up in Poland and died in the gas chambers. But in the West Bank and in Jerusalem, countless numbers of Jews where slain in Jordan's conquest of the West Bank. The unbelievable and uncalled for cruelty and hatefulness put upon the Jews by the Jordanian troops, and sanctioned by the King of Jordan is beyond description. It has been documented in many books, including Dr. W. Cleon Skousen's fine book " Fantastic Victory." The clapping of the hands and rejoicing over the devastation of the Jews among the hoards of Arabs is a reflection of that "perpetuated hate," just as we saw in the whole Muslim world as they rejoiced from Iran, Iraq, Saudi Arabia, and Palestine over the World Trade Center destruction.

Their hate for both the Jews and Americans cannot be questioned. Can we imagine that our God has not forgotten the shed blood of these hapless people, which was shed in "the time of their calamity." God's judgment is plain as we read verses 6-9.

An extremely interesting text grips our attention as we read further down the chapter. After those verses that tell of the tragedy to come when Mount Seir (or Jordan) tries to possess the Mountains of Israel, God pinpoints the real irritation as far as He is concerned. "Because thou (Jordan) has said" shows the reason why they cannot have God's favor. The rest of the verse exposes their plot against the Mountains of Israel:

"Because thou hast said, these two nations and these two countries shall be mine, and we will possess it, whereas the Lord was there."

The word for "Possess" in Hebrew is "Yarash," which literally means to seize by force--drive out and take control of. I believe this verse was fulfilled in 1948. Jordan would not accept the UN mandate to establish a homeland for the Jews in Palestine, and against all rights, by force, took possession of the Mountains of Israel. Jordan then made the boast that she would make "these two countries--mine." To their dismay, holding onto those territories became an awesome burden, precisely because "The Lord was there." Can we not see fulfillment of verse 10 in this event?

Jordan and the Palestinians are now claiming that the Jews have no historical right to the land. They are alleging that the Muslims have ever owned it. Some of their assertions from historic events which involve the past "occupation" of the land by various Gentile powers. For instance, the Egyptian Embassy in Washington put forth the idea that Jews had no link to Jerusalem advancing the idea that: "Historical facts prove that Jerusalem has witnessed Arab urban and human stability since the year 3000 BC. In 2500 BC descendants of the Jebusite Ben Canaan, made the city his capital and called it Orsalem" The text goes on to mention that in 1479 BC, the city "came under the Pharaohs " who "used to govern Palestine."

Then a significant piece of propaganda appears: "Since then, namely 600 BC, the political history of the Jews had ended in Palestine" (Jerusalem Post 12/18/00).

With this kind of logic, the Palestinians are now claiming possession of the City of Jerusalem and the West Bank by inheritance. How perfectly this fulfills what is stated in Ezekiel 36:5. Here God accuses Jordan, (the Idumeans), as having *"appointed my land into their possession."* The word "possession" here is different than the word in the 10th verse, where it means to take by force. Here it is "Morashah" which literally means, "to possess by inheritance."

Several other verses of prophecy foresee this same idea of possession. In Ezekiel 11 for instance, in speaking of the day of the Jews return from Gentile lands when they would be "gathered " and "assembled" out of the countries, (v. 17) and given the Land of Israel, verse 15 has a startling resemblance to attitudes of the Palestinians today: It speaks of those inhabiting Jerusalem in that day as saying: "Since you have gone so far from the Lord and the Land, and been gone so long, unto us is this land given in possession, (Heb, Morashah).

The Lord goes on to reveal His cause for anger against them in v. 11. Because of their envy which generated great hate against Israel:

"I will make myself known among them, (Israel), when I have judged thee. And thou shalt know that I am the Lord."

This is one of over 80 times in the book of Ezekiel where the Lord says:

"And thou shalt know that I am the Lord."

God is going to make himself known very soon. All Israel and Jordan will know that He is there, when He steps in and settles the problems over the possession of the territories, known as the West Bank, but in fact are the "Mountains of Israel." In the present peace process, liberal Jews and a secular government, first concerned with political ends and not Biblical promises, will negotiate away the territories, and yield control of Jerusalem and the Temple Mount to Jordan. Jordan in turn will yield up sovereignty to the International Community of Nations, or World

Government. All of this may be a show for peace. The only problem will be that it runs contrary to God's plan for the area. Heaven will count possession of any part of the Holy Land by any other than God's assignees, as an encroachment upon what God calls "My Land."

It will be known shortly that the *"Lord was there"* (verse 10). Verse 12 reveals God's awareness of all their *"blasphemies that they have spoken against the Mountains of Israel."* And particularly Jordan's boast: *"They are given us to consume."*

For centuries, the hate and animosity of the Arab for the Jew, and the Biblical promise concerning the Land of Israel has inspired the Muslim hoards to "consume" the land. They have burned its trees, raped its land and left total devastation. Their hate toward the God of Israel and His promise has been made very clear. In this verse their only interest in the land is to "consume" it. Verse 3 of the 36th chapter also shows their part in leaving the land desolate.

Let's especially note verse 14. *"When the whole earth* (International Community of Nations or World Government), *rejoices, I will make thee desolate."*

Right at the time when everything seems to be settled, and the International Community of Nations, backed by its Multinational forces, has *"divided the land for gain"*(Daniel 11: 39) God will step in to take possession of *"His Land."*

All of this claim to the Mountains of Israel, and the boasts of it being their land to consume, and all the blasphemies against Israel, will eventually bring God's judgment (v. 15).

In chapter 36 of Ezekiel the same subject continues. This time God is speaking to the Mountains of Israel that are personified as if they could hear and respond. *"Ye Mountains of Israel, hear the word of the Lord."* Because the enemy, (Jordan), has said against you:

"Ah even the ancient high places are ours in possession."
Here again is the claim to inheritance, (Morashah).

Among those ancient high places is, of course, the Temple Mount in Jerusalem. Jordan, to appease the UN, Europe, and Arab interests, was given continued control over the Temple Mount in Jerusalem immediately after Israel's conquest of Jerusalem in 1967. Jordan was also promised continued control over the Mount, even in the peace negotiations today. The late Rabin clearly stated the same and riled the new Palestinian Authority in Gaza and Jericho, who themselves are laying claim to Jerusalem as their capital and the Holy Mount as their rightful possession.

It is worthy to note that the terminology in the prophecies rightfully reflects Jordan's position on the Territories. At first she did not claim them by right of inheritance, or the taking of possession on historic grounds. Such claims would be futile. Nor can the "Palestinians" make any honest claim to the territories on any historic grounds. Never, by any stretch of imagination, has Jerusalem ever been a capital of any state except the State of Israel. Historically, the mountainous country known as the West Bank has been exactly as the Bible states: the "Mountains of Israel." They are not the "Mountains of Palestine" or the "Mountains of Jordan," as these would lay claim. God's intervention alone however, will clearly demonstrate this.

It is in this 5th verse however, that the gross error of the present claims to the Territories is revealed in prophecy. Let us repeat for emphasis the word "possession" here is not the same as in verse 10 of chapter 35. Rather than the word "yarash," that is "possession by force," here the word "morashah" is used. This word means to claim by inheritance.

At present, the resounding propaganda, which the world seems to be swallowing up line hook and sinker, is that the Jewish people never had a Temple on the Mount. The Jordanian Authority is allowing excavations to take place all over under the plaza of the Temple Mount, seeking to destroy all archeological evidence of Jewish presence on the Mount. While even the Koran recognized a Temple on the Mount and Jewish presence there, the Palestinian hope is that a Godless world, ignorant of Bible truths, will fall for this lie.

Today "Palestinians" have actually come from 29 different countries. Their presence in the land of Palestine, especially that portion controlled by Israel, only began when they moved there in the early part of this century to take advantage of jobs created by Jewish businesses which where beginning to flourish in Israel. Any historic claim by these people to the land is contrary to history. In the late 1800s, as we have earlier shown, the land was totally desolate. No one, including the shepherds, lived there. Ezekiel 36, verse 3 clearly foresees this very condition. The Lord says: *"Because they have made you* (Mountains of Israel) *desolate."* Because of this forsaken condition of the land, these people came in and *"swallowed you up on every side,"* thus clearly prophesying claim to the land by all the countries *"around about"* (verse 4).

My point is this: only Israel and the Jews, the seed of Abraham, can historically lay claims to the Land, and the City of Jerusalem as a capital of their State, and especially the Temple Mount. Note in verse 6 God clearly associates the Mountains of Israel with the "Land of Israel." He continues in verse 7: *"The heathen that are about you, they shall bear their shame."*

In Ezekiel 36 verse 8 expositions begin that leave no doubt about the time frame of all of these prophecies. They are set in the days of Israel's return to the Land from Diaspora. In the next few verses of this chapter we have clear prophecies of the rebuilding of the land by the returned Jews. It is my honest conviction that, in spite of present peace initiatives and promise of autonomy for the Mountains of Israel, that the Israelis will continue to settle the West Bank. These prophecies certainly support that conclusion.

> *Yield your fruit, oh Mountains of Israel, to my people Israel, for they are at hand* (v.8).
> *I am for you, the Lord says, and will return to you* (v. 9).

The population of Jews on the West Bank will continue to increase, also according to verse 10. Cities will be inhabited and waste places built. Verse 11 makes another revealing prophecy: *"I will settle you after your old estates."*

This statement clearly harks back to the former tribal arrangements that must assuredly include the Mountains of Israel in the new Nation of Israel. During the days of Joshua and the Judges, the twelve tribes of Israel were allotted certain areas of the land. These allotments included all of the present West Bank. Verse 12 declares the Mountains of Israel, or West Bank to be the inheritance of Israel, and its future possession. According to this prophecy, the old estates will be allotted again.

The reason for the scattering of the people of Israel, their return and the occupation in the last days of the land is once again confirmed in the next verses. God's promise to restore the land and the people comes into view again in verse 24. At that time Israel will be sprinkled, a reflection back to the temple cleansing. A "new heart" and a "new spirit" are given them. God will put his spirit back in them (v.28) and God will make the Mountains of Israel under their care, like the Garden of Eden (v.35).

Chapter 37 contains more predictions on Israel's new birth, resurrection, and return in the great analogy of Ezekiel's bone yard, picturing in dramatic terms Israel's return. It also sees both the House of Judah, and the House of Israel combined together in one nation. Again the Spirit is quick to confirm their unified nation to include the Mountains of Israel, or the West Bank:

> *"And I will make them one nation in the land upon the Mountains of Israel."*

Today, true to these prophecies, we see all of the tribes of Israel represented and united in the Modern State of Israel.

Verse 25 confirms the earlier covenant made with Jacob and gives them all the land promised to Him. Verse 26 speaks of a new "covenant" that will allow for the building of the Temple again. Of course, if the Temple is to be rebuilt, it cannot be built other than on the Holy Mount. Thus the situation in the Middle East is far from settled.

ISRAEL FORCED INTO BOGUS PEACE

Israel is being forced into a bogus peace with known terrorists. They are being forced to give away land rightly promised them. This is clearly contrary to God's plan for the territories.   Mr. Perez envisioned a confederation between Israel and Jordan with a Palestinian State. "Everybody knows this is the solution," he said in a recent interview with the *Jerusalem Post* (12/11/93).

In the Declaration Text of the Peace initiative, Rabin promised to: "Vigorously continue negotiations to arrive at a state of peace, based on Security Council Resolutions 242 and 338 in all their aspects, and founded on freedom, equality and justice."

It will be recalled that these resolutions demand a complete withdrawal from the West Bank, Golan and Gaza. It is clear by the above statement, that Mr. Rabin intends to give back all of these territories. In doing so he was contrary to God's plan. The *Jerusalem Post* stated: "International community will opt for a Jordanian-Israeli solution for the future of the territories" (August 6,'94).

Remember Ezekiel 35:10: *"Because thou hast said, these two nations and these two countries shall be mine, and we will possess it..."* These negotiations may be right by international law, or by the world community, but they are not right by the Lord. In Joel 3:2, God clearly declares that he has a problem with the people who *"parted my land."* And in Amos 1:13 we read concerning Jordan, here called

Amman:

> *I will not turn away the punishment thereof; because they have---enlarged their border.*

It is obvious both by prophecy and by diplomatic process in the area at present, that Jordan and Israel will be forced into an agreement over the West Bank. It is also obvious by prophecy that Israel must eventually possess the Mountains of Israel.

Mohammed Jadallah, of the Democratic Front for the Liberation of Palestine, in the *Jerusalem Post* for August 6, 1994 said: "...to pressure Arafat into accepting a confederation of the territories with Jordan."

Any serious negotiations over the Temple Mount in Jerusalem must include Jordan.

It is they who control the Temple Mount, and Israel is committed to allow them to continue control, even though King Hussein had long recognized God's right to the Temple Mount and Israel's right to exist. In the Declaration Text, number 3, Mr. Rabin states:

> "....Hashimite Kingdom of Jordan is Muslim holy shrines in Jerusalem. When negotiations on the permanent status will take place, Israel will give high priority to the Jordanian historic role in these shrines...promote interfaith relations among the three monotheistic religions."

In 1948, when Israel was ready to declare independence, and Golda Meir knew the Arabs would attack from all sides, she decided to face King Abdullah of Jordan. King Abdullah is the late King Hussein's grandfather. At the risk of her life, she met King Abdullah in Jordan. There she pled with him on Israel's behalf. He was sympathetic, but said he had no choice. Golda reminded him that the Jews were his only friends. He replied:

"I know that; I have no illusions; I believe with all my heart that divine providence has brought you back here, restoring you, a Semitic people who were exiled in Europe."

King Hussein told the *Jerusalem Post* that he could see no reason why the Jews should not be allowed to build their Temple on the Holy Mount. In an August 6th edition of the *Jerusalem Post*, Hussein said:

"For many, many years and with every prayer I have asked God the Almighty to help me be a part of forging peace between the children of Abraham as Moslems; For the word Islam means submitting to the one God. This is a dream that those before me had - my dead grandfather and now I. To feel that we are close to fulfilling that dream and presenting future generations in our region with a legacy of hope and openness, where normality is that which replaces the abnormal in our lives;

which unfortunately, over the years has become normal: Where neighbors meet: Where people meet; Where human relations thrive; Where all seek with their tremendous talents a better future and a better tomorrow."

REASONS WHY THE JORDANIAN PEACE WILL HOLD

In closing this chapter, I would like to briefly explain why I personally believe the Jordanian peace effort will last. Not that it eliminates God's judgment upon the country for their hate to Israel, for those judgments have come and will come. I do believe, however, that the peace agreement between Israel and Jordan does set the stage for fulfillment of certain prophecies. Let me briefly enumerate them.

1. Jordan controls the Temple Mount.

I believe it will hold because of Jordan's control over the Mount at this time. Israel will have to compromise if ever the international community of nations is to add its sanctions. This seems to agree with a projection in the Book of Revelation, chapter 11. When the Tribulation Temple is measured, i.e. for rebuilding, John is instructed to leave out the Court of the Gentiles which would be:

"given unto the Gentiles, and the Holy City shall they tread under foot forty two months."

In this text, it is obvious that both Jews and Gentiles during the Tribulation will share the Temple Mount. It also shows that the part of the Mount occupied by the "Gentiles" will be the area of the court which was "without the Temple." The court, which was outside of the Temple proper in the Old Temple set-up, was known as the Court of the Gentiles, and lay just South of the Temple proper. The Dome of the Rock occupies this area today. It is the third Holiest place in the Muslim world, and is the point of controversy at the present time.

It would seem then that these verses in Revelation 11 certainly foresee the very scenario that exists on the Temple Mount today. The Gentile Muslims are in control of the whole area, and if the Jews are ever given right to build their Temple, it will be built to the North of the Dome of the Rock. Much work has been done to date by several scholars in Israel, to demonstrate that the actual site of the earlier Temple was in fact directly in line with the Eastern Gate. The Holy of Holies would, according to them, be under the little Monument, (known as the Monument to the Word & Spirit) which the author believes is commemorative of the 10 Commandments in the Ark of the Covenant and the Shekinah Glory. It sits just a little West and North of the Dome and is in line with the Eastern Gate.

According to these scholars, The Temple could be

built on its original site without disturbing the Dome of the Rock. The peace process between Israel and Jordan is setting up this exact situation. It is also the only arrangement that will satisfy the International Community. Thus, the Jordan peace initiative seems to be scheduled to hold, at least through the Tribulation.

2. Jordan is the only country to escape the Antichrist.

In the words of prophecy, Jordan will evidently escape the Antichrist's control. According to Daniel 11:4, Edom, Moab and Amman will not be taken into the Antichrist scheme:

> "He, (Antichrist) *shall enter also into the glorious land,* (The Holy Land) *and many countries shall be overthrown; but these shall escape out of his hand, even Edom, Moab, and the chief of the Children of Amman."*

From this text it seems clear to us that Jordan, as the modern country that inhabits the old countries of Edom, Moab and Amman, will not be found among the conquests of the Antichrist. Our next paragraph may give the reason.

3. Jordan will hide Israel from the Antichrist during last part of the Tribulation.

We have a most amazing prediction in the book of Isaiah. Chapter 15 exposes us to God's burden for Moab.

Among all the areas included in this burden is Nebo, Heshbon, Elealeth, Jahaz and others. All of these are within the modern borders of Jordan. Verse 5 finds God's heart crying out for Moab's "fugitives." These "fugitives" are the subject of chapter 16. Verse 1 sees the lamb sent to the ruler of the land, (Jordan) and in verse 3 Jordan is exhorted to "take counsel, execute judgment." All of this is in relationship to the command from God that they are to:

"hide the outcasts; bewray not him that wandereth."

Who are these "outcasts"? Verse 4 gives the answer: *Let mine outcasts dwell with thee, Moab; be thou a covert to them from the face of the spoiler; for the extortioner is at an end, the spoiler ceaseth, the oppressors are consumed out of the land.*

(See also Psalms 60:8-12, which agrees with this prophecy.)

Here we see that the outcasts are God's people. They have fled to Moab, and are to be protected there from the *"spoiler, extortioner, and oppressor."* These terms we understand to describe the Antichrist and his cruel reign.

When we relate these texts to two other scriptural references, we can clearly see the scenario. In Matthew 24, Jesus warns the people of Judea to flee into the wilderness when they see the *"Abomination of Desolation standing in the Holy Place"* (v.15,16). This, we believe is a reference to the time when the Antichrist sits in the Temple claiming to be God (I1 Thessalonians 2:4). Thus we see that the righteous Jews will need to flee from the face of the Antichrist for a short time while he rules from a throne on the Holy Mount. He is called *"spoiler, extortioner, and oppressor."* In Revelation 12, we are again told that those Jews that have a testimony of Jesus in the last days will have to flee from the Dragon (Satan)(Revelation 12:14). Satan will inhabit the Antichrist in those days. All this will take place in the middle of the Tribulation (Daniel 9:27).

By our text in Daniel 11, and Isaiah 16, it is clear that the place of their refuge will be the Kingdom of Jordan, in the area of "Sela." Sela can be shown to be the ancient red rose city of Petra.

4. Because the International Community of Nations will demand it.

We have quoted before, but it bears repeating here, the statement from the *Jerusalem Post* for August 6th 1994:

"The International Community will opt for a Jordanian-Israeli solution for the future of the territories."

For a time prior to the Tribulation, and finally the coming of the Lord, an international solution will be sought. This will include the internationalizing of Jerusalem, allowing joint and equal access of all of the religions of Abraham's children to the Mount of Abraham. This will include all of the Monotheistic religions of the world, namely Christianity, Muslim, and Judaism.

Since the Crusaders of Europe established a throne on the South end of the Mount, and the Muslims have well set their claim to the central part of the Mount, namely the site of the Dome; and since it is becoming clearer that the site of the Holiest can be shown to be at the North end of the Mount, it seems we see a scenario developing. It will seem logical to the World Community of Nations that the Mount should be divided three ways, giving all of the religions free access to their area.

International Christendom may be allowed to set up a center on the South, the Muslims would be allowed the area of the Dome of the Rock. The Jews would be allowed to build their Temple on the northern end. Thus the mount would be compromised nicely to accommodate all those interested.

To the liberal and agnostic Jews, this arrangement will seem acceptable, and will seem to answer the problem. To the Torah Faithful, however, it will be an abomination. Their uprising may precipitate the very persecution spoken of in the 12th Chapter of Zechariah and also the 12th chapter of Revelation. An International Multi-national force, then under control of the Beast and empowered by the Dragon, would be employed to put down the rebellion. This faithful remnant would then have to flee into the wilderness.

(Isaiah 16, Daniel 11, Matthew 24, and Revelation 12) At that same time Michael would be dispatched from Heaven to come to the aid of the outcasts. A time of terrible Tribulation would follow. Angelic forces would protect the fleeing faithful from the face of the Dragon, the Beast, and their international forces under control of the Antichrist.

There is another scenario, which is presenting itself. There are around 144,000 settlers on the West Bank. When and if the West Bank is ever established as an independent Palestinian State, these settlers will be in dire danger. When the Antichrist takes over by breaking the Covenant, which no doubt would include some arrangement concerning the settlers of the West Bank, these settlers will be forced to flee. This agrees perfectly with Jesus' own words in Matthew 24:15, where he says that they that are in Judea will have to flee. Remember that Judea is part of the West Bank.

In the end, the Lamb will be sent to the "fugitives" in Petra, and with the Church, would meet the Antichrist forces first in the Valley of Jehoshaphat, and finally in Megiddo. Having defeated Hell's forces and all nations that fight against Jerusalem, the Lord will return to Zion (Zechariah 8:2,3).

Thus saith the Lord of hosts; I was jealous for Zion with great jealousy, and I was jealous for her with great fury.

Thus saith the Lord; I am returned unto Zion, and will dwell in the midst of Jerusalem; and Jerusalem shall be called the city of truth; and the mountain of the Lord of hosts, the holy mountain.

AMEN (SO BE IT LORD)

CHAPTER 3

JERUSALEM
AND IT'S IMPORTANCE

JERUSALEM IS NOT NEGOTIABLE

If you could visit Jerusalem today, you may be invited to take the short but steep descent down the face of Olivet, which leads from Mt Olivet's brow, to the Brook Kedron near the Garden of Gathsemane. About halfway into your journey down the face of the Mount, you may want to take a side path prepared for visitors. At the sight where tradition says Jesus cried over Jerusalem, you might want to rest in the shade to meditate on His sorrow as he wept over Jerusalem: *"Oh Jerusalem, Jerusalem,"* he cried (Matthew 23:37), *"If you, even you, had only known, on this day, what would bring you peace, but now they are hidden from you"* (Luke 19:42, NIV).

As you read these passages at that spot, there seems to

be a lingering sense of the same sorrow and deep concern which the spirit of our Lord has left there. Today Jerusalem, (Jehovah brings peace) has certainly had it's share of the world's trouble. And even though we have found in over a score of trips to the city, an atmosphere of peace there, only to listen to any headlines today, will tell you that Jerusalem is a long way from what the Lord had hoped for the city.

The Jews are certainly putting Jerusalem in jeopardy. They are not moving toward a lasting peace, but rather a bogus peace. This is because they are yet a secular state, and not able to cast their reliance upon the great God of Israel who alone is able to deliver them, and bring them the peace of which Jesus spoke. By trusting in their own strength they are putting the State of Israel in harm's way. Also by reliance upon the World Community of Nations for their existence, they are therefore under duress to negotiate away the Mountains of Israel, and the Golan. Such a move would place their troops at great disadvantage and would weaken their military strength, by putting avowed enemies in potentially advantageous positions. More seriously they would be acting contrary to God's will. With the West Bank as an autonomous State, Israel would only be 11 miles wide in its center. This narrow stretch of coastal plain is directly under the high places of the Mountains to the East, making it very vulnerable to attack.

That is why they want to construct a wall along the borders between Israel proper and the West Bank in this area. It is the only way they see to protect the vulnerable Plains of Sharon from military intrusion, as well as to prevent suicide bombers from crossing the border.

Any negotiation that gives away the West Bank makes an extremely hazardous situation for Jerusalem, and also puts them in direct opposition to God's final solution. The peace negotiations can only take them farther from their goal, which is to make Jerusalem their capital city. These negotiations also serve to encourage terrorists in their own goals. Not understanding democratic process and free societies, the Muslims see these agreements as a sign of weakness and compromise only to be used as steps toward their final goal; the total destruction of the State of Israel.

By negotiating with Jordan for control of the Temple Mount, and the Mountains of Israel, the Jews move farther from God's goal in the area. All of this serves only to put Jerusalem on the front burner of international affairs. As we have shown, all these diplomacies are not moving toward peace, but in fact, setting the world up for its final battle.

It will only be at a time in Israel's desperation, when all of the International Community, including America, has forsaken her and she stands alone, with another holocaust imminent, that Israel will:

Blow ye the trumpet, sound an alarm in my holy mountain.... Sanctify a fast, call a solemn assembly; gather the people, sanctify the congregation (Joel 2:1, 15, 16).

It seems here that Israel finally turns to her source, and casts her total reliance upon the God of old. Then and only then, will Israel have abiding peace. In the meantime a temporary and false peace is in the making.

Because of the explosive situation in the Middle East, and its potential for world war, the United States and the UN are both very interested in these affairs. With no care or knowledge of God and His plan for the area, they proceed to force their policies on the tiny State of Israel, and the Arab States around it. Thus, what was nothing but a heap of rubble in the midst of a barren desert inhabited by a very few only decades ago, has now become the focal point of world diplomacy. Prior to our time no one could ever have imagined Jerusalem could come to the forefront on the world scene.

I will state my conclusions again. The peace process is a bogus peace because, (1) it is built upon false hopes and confused diplomacy, (2) because it runs contrary to God's will and plans for the area, (3) it does not settle the issue of Jerusalem. Until the Jerusalem problem is settled there can never be peace in the area (4) It negotiates away the Mountains of Israel, which is a portion of the Promised Land to fall to Israel. All of this makes any covenant or negotiations over Jerusalem extremely interesting to those of us who study Bible Prophecy.

It is incredible to notice also, that at the very time when the Hamas, Intifada, Jihad, and other extremist groups are encouraged to keep up their terrorism, in hope of making Jerusalem their Capital City, the Jews worldwide have written, and circulated a document which declares Jerusalem forever their own Capital, and the Capital of the State of Israel. There appears to be much duplicity among the Jewish Statesmen, who on the one hand, declare "Jerusalem is not negotiable," and that Jerusalem, united and whole will always be the Capital of the State of Israel. On the other hand they promise to negotiate Jerusalem in final settlement. This Covenant, called the "Jerusalem Covenant," will be explored in the next chapter.

Have you noticed that when any Jewish Statesman gets close to any final status which would negotiate away any part of Jerusalem, he is removed. It was after hammering the Knesset pulpit and screaming that he did not believe in Biblical Israel or the Biblical promise, that Mr. Rabin was murdered. It happened just three days later and was by the hand of an Hesidic Jew.

So let us explore a bit further the Jerusalem Covenant, made and signed by the Sanhedrin to the Jews worldwide, and also most of the Heads of State in Israel. While we deal with the Covenant of Jerusalem, let us see what the Prophetic Scriptures have to say of Jerusalem in the last days.

JERUSALEM AND WORLD JEWRY

There can be no question of the Biblical promise of Israel's return to the land, city and finally to the Mount. In the face of gigantic odds, with a world and it's Empires dead set against the Jews worldwide and with the political and diplomatic possibilities hard set against there ever again being a State called "Israel," and with the Holy Land completely in control of a formidable power totally set against any hope of a Jewish return, the fact is that the Jews have returned and there is a State called Israel, and Jerusalem is in their hands.

Even the predominant Christian community had become their enemy. In the early 4th century, when the Catholic Church proposed to be the Universal Church, it was taught that God had given up on the Jews. They would never again exist as a people and all the promises of restoration of the Land were to the Church. This was the teaching which insighted the Crusades, one of Christianity's greatest embarrassments. Even many of the early reformers picked up this error. The doctrine came to be known as "Replacement Theology."

If those who have taught the Replacement Theology theory had been correct in their understanding of God's plan for the Jew, no doubt long ago the Jews would be assimilated into the nations, and there would be no more urgency over Jerusalem. The church, living in the hope of the New Jerusalem and Heaven, would no longer have any more interest in Jerusalem than any other historical spot. There would be no Jewish hope and all Bible promises would be fulfilled in the Church.

However, the Jews are very much alive and for two thousand years, scattered throughout the world since the overthrow of Jerusalem by the Roman army in AD 70, the Orthodox faithful have coveted Jerusalem as their dream and hope. When celebrating the Feast of Pentecost, for instance, at the end of the celebration each family will run outside, face toward Jerusalem, and say: "Next year, Jerusalem."

Then they will refer to their hope in the scriptures, such as Psalms 122:

Let us go into the house of the Lord. Our feet shall stand within thy gates, O Jerusalem.

...Pray for the peace of Jerusalem; they shall prosper that love thee...

Because of the house of the Lord our God, I will seek thy good.

In ceremony, they will quote from Psalm 137:6:

If I do not remember thee, let my tongue cleave to the roof of my mouth; if I prefer not Jerusalem above my chief joy.

Why did they refer to such scriptures, and even now rely upon those same promises, when they were so far and so long removed from Jerusalem? How have they kept their hope alive, when for centuries they have been citizens of other countries, and Jerusalem has been nothing but a heap? It is because of their hope in God's faithfulness and promise,

> *"The Lord doth build up Jerusalem; He gathereth the outcasts of Israel. Praise ye the Lord, O Jerusalem, Praise thy God, O Zion"* (Psalm 147:2, 12).

They know that God has said he will not rest until Jerusalem shines in righteousness and glory. (Isaiah 62:1-2) God has promised to rebuild Jerusalem in the last days and establish it. He is to make it the joy of the last day's return of the Jews to the land of promise:

> *I create Jerusalem a rejoicing, and her people a joy; And I will rejoice over Jerusalem, and joy in my people* (Isaiah 65:18,19).

Is it any wonder then, when Jerusalem fell back into Israel's control in the Six Day War of June 1967, that such joy broke out in world Jewry? In Jerusalem, right in the midst of battle, Jewish soldiers threw down their weapons and ran for the Western Wall. A revival broke out there.

One of the most touching stories of the 1948 War of Independence, comes to us in the prologue of a very exciting and inspiring book written by Larry Collins and Dominique Lapierre, entitled *O Jerusalem*. The Jewish hope for the re-establishment of their heritage in the land of promise, and their return to Jerusalem as their own beloved city, had never been so close. They had kept the Sabbath and conformed to every precept of the Law. They had memorized their Torah verses, and kept careful watch over the Scriptures for centuries. Daily they had prayed for the City of David, and beseeched the God of Abraham to bring His people back to Zion and Jerusalem.

As the last of the British soldiers were leaving Jerusalem, hopeful eyes peered from every window and around every wall. Their ancestors had watched other armies move out in past times; the Assyrians, Babylonians, Greeks, Romans, Byzantines, Persians, Mamelukes, Arabs, Crusaders and the Turks. Now the Allied forces, which had occupied the land and city since the end of WWII were leaving, and on the morrow, armistice was to be established. It was the eve of Israel's independence. Could they actually hope that finally, after nearly two millennium, they were to have their most longed-for dreams fulfilled?

Suddenly, as the last column of British soldiers were about to exit the city, they veered left up a cobblestone alley, stopped in front of the arched stone crowning at entry to No.3, on Chayim Street. A British Colonel stepped forward and knocked on the door.

Inside Rabbi Mordechai Weingarten, senior citizen of the Jewish Quarter in Jerusalem, put on his black vest and jacket, adjusted his black hat, pushed up his spectacles, and stepped to the door to greet the Colonel. From the right hand of the Colonel dangled a large bar of rusted iron almost a foot long. With a solemn gesture he offered to the Rabbi the key to Zion's Gate. The key was considered to be the Key to the City of Jerusalem. Handing the keys to the Rabbi, he said:

"From the year 70 AD until today, a key to the gates of Jerusalem has never been in Jewish hands. This is the first time in eighteen centuries that your people have been so privileged."

When the Roman Emperor Titus destroyed the city and the Temple, it's despairing priests had thrown the keys to Jerusalem toward Heaven crying, "...God, henceforth be thou the guardian of the keys."

Now that Key was to be put back in the hands of God's ancient people.

When the old priest had received the key, he muttered in a low worshipful voice, with his eyes toward heaven:

"Blessed art Thou, O Lord, who has granted us life and sustenance and permitted us to reach this day."

Then addressing the Colonel, he said, "I accept this key in the name of my people."

The Colonel stood at attention and saluted. After an admonition that their parting be as friends, and a good luck and goodbye, he turned and marched the rest of his soldiers out of the city. As the old priest turned to close the door, the noise of gunfire, sinister and terrifying, began to rise from every quarter of the city (*O Jerusalem, Prologue*).

JERUSALEM THE PRIZE

Given the kind of price that has been paid to win Jerusalem, and the 18 centuries of hope and prayers of the Jewish people, it has been hard to understand how Rabin and the Israeli Government could be so quick to negotiate away it's future. It is especially hard to understand how they can so readily return control of the Temple Mount to Jordan, except that we understand the pressure being put upon them by the International Community. One thing is clear. No peace negotiation is worth the paper it is written on until it settles the issue of Jerusalem. Rabin and Arafat had no sooner signed the Oslo treaty, and the ink dry, before Jerusalem came to the forefront. Three days after the signing, Arafat claimed Jerusalem as the new capital of the Palestinian State.

"JERUSALEM SHALL BE THE CAPITAL OF THE PALESTINIAN STATE"

No Palestinian State existed, of course, but Arafat was already laying claim to the same. He admits he saw the peace initiative as the first step to the formulation of a

Palestinian State. He also admits he saw it as the first step to the destruction of the Jewish State.

Such acute controversy has arisen as to bring on what seems to be a world crisis. President Bill Clinton, together with Mr. Barak, Prime Minister of Israel, tried so hard to settle the West Bank problem. At the Wye Conference and under Clinton's prompting and pressure, the Prime Minister of Israel came near to promising a give-away of everything possible, except Jerusalem. However, when the subject of Jerusalem came up, the whole deal fell through. Bill Clinton invited Yasser Arafat, (who had been driven into exile out of Lebanon in 1982, and had been completely out of the picture for over 10 years), back into the negotiations. Again the old antagonist of Israel refused to agree to anything less than all of Jerusalem and would not settle for anything less. Mr. Barak would have to sacrifice everything including Jerusalem. This he could not do and keep the confidence of the people of Israel. Earlier at Oslo, Yitzak Rabin dared not touch the Jerusalem problem, and Sharon Perez was dumped for suggesting that Jerusalem be internationalized, and put under the direct administration of the Pope of Rome. Netanyahu, then Prime Minister of Israel, affirmed without question that "Jerusalem is not negotiable." Now of late, Present George W. Bush and Tony Blair, are making the same error by promoting a Palestinian State through their "Road Map." No sooner had it been initiated until we could see it falter and hear the rattles of it's death thralls.

The U.E. is almost totally anti-Israel, with only 6 seats of the 626 seat Parliament being pro-Israel. It is pro-Palestinian, yet it has not dared to touch Jerusalem. England remains neutral, and slightly pro-Palestinian, although it was originally their mandate that started the movement toward a homeland for the Jews. The UN has had several resolutions on the table since 1948-50, yet they have not dared to force Israel to exercise any one of them. Kissinger would liked to have pushed for the exercise of the UN resolutions and forced Israel to internationalize Jerusalem, and the Pope even hinted in private that he might make Jerusalem the new Rome. But none of these have dared to bring the subject to serious negotiations. Hesidim of the Jews expects to have all of Jerusalem some day in the age of the Messiah, but is willing to compromise the subject at present. The Temple Faithful have tried year after year to place a cornerstone for the future Temple, only to be turned back by the Israeli forces. Until the issue is settled, the United States will not move its Embassy to Jerusalem even though a by-partisan resolution was unanimously passed during the Clinton years to do so.

Such controversy can be shown in the following quotes from various sources:

PLO hard-liner Farrouk Kaddoumi reported the same

to the *Jerusalem Post* (8/6/94):

"The Palestinian Covenant, calling for destruction of the Jewish State of Israel will not be changed."

Mr. Rabin responded to these remarks:

"A United Jerusalem is the defacto Capital of the State of Israel.." (Ibid)

In the agreement with Jordan, Rabin showed his pragmatism when he said:

"Israel respects the present special rule of the Hashamite Kingdom of Jordan in the Muslim Holy Places in Jerusalem."

This agreement with Jordan brought immediate reaction from the radical faction of the Arabs:

"Who gave Israel right to decide who has rights in the Islamic Institutions in Jerusalem?" (Farrouk Kaddoumi, *Jeremiah Post*, 8/6/94).

Chief Rabbi Yesrael Meir Lau spoke for the Jewish community:

"Hussein is welcome but Jerusalem is ours."

An East Jerusalem Palestinian Paper, Al-Kuds, Reported on August 13, '94:

"Jerusalem must be under Palestinian control,

politically and religiously."

However, Mr. Rabin storms:
"Jerusalem is the Capital of Israel forever"
(*Jeremiah Post*, 6/11/'94).

Now, Mr. Arafat is not convinced, for he becomes almost ferocious when he declares:
"We will go to Jerusalem, Jerusalem, Jerusalem to pray there together."

Israel's response:
"Jerusalem, never, never, never..." (*Jeremiah Post* 8/6/ '94)

In big bold signs we see these words throughout Israel:
"Jerusalem is not negotiable" (Torah Times).

At the same time it is clearly spelled out in all of the peace documents that Jerusalem will come up for negotiations in the future.

We give you the previous information to demonstrate how explosive the issue of Jerusalem is, and why no peace accord is valid without settling this issue. It is probably accurate to say that there is nothing in the making today that is about to settle the Jerusalem question. That is why we are sure this situation is exactly what was meant by the prophecy in chapters 12 and 14 of Zechariah. There we are told that Jerusalem would become a *"cup of trembling"* and a *"burdensome stone"* to all nations around about.

Jesus knew this when He wept over Jerusalem in His day, as He anticipated by foreknowledge the very days we are living in:

> *"O Jerusalem, Jerusalem, if you only knew, at the eleventh hour, on what your peace depends, but you cannot see it."*

This is as much a prophecy for the end time as it was for His day. It not only anticipated the devastation of Jerusalem just 40 years later, but also foresees an end time scenario when Jerusalem once again will be under siege (Zechariah14:2).

Today, as we move into the final end-time setting, it is Jerusalem again which is seeking peace. If Jerusalem only knew today upon what it's real peace depends on, it would not be so quick to trade off land which God has designated to be it's security for the last days. We must ask why Jerusalem is so important as to make the whole world tremble?

JERUSALEM'S IMPORTANCE

What is it that makes a city so important to the world, when just half a century ago, it was mostly rubble on a heap of 26 destroyed civilizations, surrounded by nothing but desolation? London, yes; Berlin, Paris, Rome, Washington, Tokyo, or Moscow yes, but Jerusalem? This question is most baffling to the world's strategists. They who do not consider God and His Word of any importance or consequence today, are hard put to answer this question.

A world that has for the past 50 years tried to eradicate religion from its midst, or at the least, ignore it, are faced more than ever with God and His Bible. A United Nations, which for half a century has tried to shun religion and hoping it would go away, now finds its greatest challenges involving religion: the Catholics and Protestants in Ireland, the Catholics and Buddhists in southeast Asia, the Jews and Muslims in the Middle East, to name a few. Religion, which was to gradually disappear, now is on the front burner of world politics. In the United States, where Liberals have tried to stem its influence for the most part of this century, find today their greatest challenge in the "Religious Right." They grow increasingly exasperated in their effort to totally secularize the nation. While Buddhism, Hinduism and other Far Eastern cults invade America through something called the New Age, three powerful monotheistic religions come to the forefront of world diplomacy. Those three monotheistic religions are the players in the Jerusalem conflict today.

It is easy to see why Jerusalem is so important to each of these as to put the world in jeopardy and retain their interest there:

1. TO THE WORLD ORDER - THE COMMUNITY OF NATIONS

In case you have not kept up on world events, it might be a surprise to you that we should confess that the New World Order is already here. Oh, it has a ways to go before it can exercise it's full prophetic proportions, but it is here. It's main visible body politic is of course the UN, but it is already working in the Trilateral of three power blocks of nations, namely the United States, the European Community, and Japan. These three powers, along with the rest of the world, are controlled by the International Monetary Fund and other world entities of the International Banking cartels. They control world economy, while most of the world politics is now strongly influenced by the United Nations.

Since the Gulf War, where the Multinational Forces were born, a world army is being developed. Many of our Armed Forces are being trained under foreign commanders and a foreign flag. They are committed to fight under a foreign command, even against the United States if necessary. Within the boundaries of our great nation, foreign troops are being trained to confront us, take our guns and subject us to a foreign power, namely the UN.

This is precisely what President Bush Sr. meant on the day that troops began to be dispatched to the Gulf. While standing on the lawn of the Institute of International Affairs in Aspen, Colo., he used for the first time in public the term "New World Order," when he said: "This is the beginning of the New World Order."

George W. Bush, like his father is a committed "Internationalist, howbeit not a "Globalist."

The new "Coalition" formed to combat terror is only another step toward a world army. With the world political machinery nearly complete, a world economy in place, and the ICC (International Criminal Court) in session since July 1, 2002. All of the ingredients for a world government are virtually here. The "Beast" of Revelation is well on its way. The Devil's plans through the Gentile Nations for the city of Jerusalem is foreshadowed in all of the present day events. Because Satan is the "God of this world," his own hate toward the plan and purpose of God for the Jews and their land is being fledged out and expressed in the heart of the International Community.

The good hope of a war-ravished world for an age of world-wide peace, might in fact be realized at this time if it were not for so many ungodly planners who do not know God's ultimate plans and who keep running contrary to Him. Having set themselves up as the peacekeepers of the world, it makes it necessary that they involve themselves in the Middle East. Inadvertently, they are actually setting the World Community up for it's final affront with God. As Mr. de Coursey Jr., editor of "Intelligence Digest," has said, "What is happening in the Middle East is going to bring the world to its last battle."

Were it not for the Jerusalem problem, and the Middle East crisis causing it, the world's planners might be realizing their long-envisioned peace. It probably would not be, but to hear them say it- Jerusalem is the only thing that is standing in the way of world peace today. So in their minds, they must settle the Jerusalem problem.

Without the slightest clue, the world is playing right into God's prophetic picture. Since the world has decided to turn it's back on God, they are destined by divine decree to meet God in the Middle East. God has declared his determination to bring them there that he might deal with them (Zephaniah 3:8). In Zechariah 12:2,3. and 14:2, God plainly says their gathering in the Middle East will be His plan and doings. In Joel 3:9-12 and Micah 4:1-3, and Revelation 16:14-16, He shows His plan to judge the world of nations in the Holy Land. Even if the world did not desire to be involved, it's fate is set. There are very powerful forces working with great international interest in the Middle East. Oil interests have forced the industrial nations to buddy up to the Arab Cartels. Israel's mandate by the UN with America's, Britain's, and Canada's blessings has made it necessary that the World Community be involved.

THE DEVIL'S DOINGS

It has become apparent to world diplomacy, that a peaceful settlement of the Jerusalem problem will be necessary before the World Order can come to full fruition. And what will be the world's answer? Internationalize Jerusalem, of course. When they enter into a covenant with Israel and the Arab nations to put Jerusalem under the World Order, they are inadvertently setting up a world leader to sit on a throne in Jerusalem.

Eventually, under full direction of the Devil himself, that's exactly what will happen (2 Thessalonians 2:4). Not only have the Jewish and Muslim powers set Jerusalem as a priority, but so has the Devil in his coming bid for world rule.

The World Community will not recognize the Devil, nor realize it is he who is exercising his will through them, so it will be very easy for him, (from their blind side), to manipulate them right into his plan. So, precisely according to prophetic pattern, the World Community is forcing an agreement over Jerusalem, and that often hinted at and openly spoken of Covenant is about to be "confirmed."

2. TO THE CHRISTIANS

Arafat is playing heavily on the "Christians" for support against the Jews in obtaining control of Jerusalem. Let us not be deceived. Yassar Arafat has no more respect for Christian holy places than for the Jewish shrines. I witnessed this during the Lebanon Campaign in 1982. I was privileged to accompany the Israeli troops up the coast all the way to Beirut. There I saw signs everywhere of Arafat's "care" for the Christian holy places. The Christians of Lebanon were slaughtered by thousands, and every church building that fell under the PLO's control, was burned, gutted, and used as a PLO hideout. The Christian's best advantage would be the Jews, given the choice between them, Arafat, or the Muslims. The Christian community in Bethlehem has certainly discovered that they were far better off under Israel's care than under Arafat's control as they are at the present time.

As for Evangelical Christians, what should be our special interest in Jerusalem? As we have stated before, the Christian should have no earthly city, for we look for one to come. Many have tried to give the Christians a central city on earth. For instance; the Catholic Church trying to make Rome their capital city. However, Paul clearly teaches that we have no "continuing city." (Hebrews 13:14, 12:22,23):

> For here have we no continuing city, but we seek one to come...but we are come unto mount Sion, and unto the city of the living God, the heavenly Jerusalem, and to an innumerable company of angels. To the general assembly of the firstborn, which are written in heaven, and to God the Judge of all, and to the spirits of just men made perfect.

There are other interests to the Christian concerning

the city of Jerusalem. For instance, God has promised peace to those who love and pray for the peace of her (Psalm 122:6). It is also important to us because of it's special interest to our Lord. He wept over it, he died there, was resurrected there, and will return there on his homecoming day (Zechariah14:4). The Holy Spirit brought the church to birth there, and we are going to meet our Lord there in the day of his triumphal entry. Jesus will rule in the Millennium from there, (Isaiah 24:23) and the Church will celebrate the Feast of Tabernacles there throughout the millennium (Isaiah 27:13, and Zechariah 14:16).

However, there is a more fundamental reason. It is my persuasion that Evangelical Christians should be most interested in the events surrounding Jerusalem, the Temple Mount, and the Holy Land, for a real and practical purpose. It is of utmost importance to us Christians that every detail of prophecy concerning the Jews and their land be fulfilled, simply because the integrity of our God depends on it. If God is a God of his Word, and if he is omnipotent (and He is) therefore big enough to fulfill His Word (no matter what circumstances exist) then He can be depended upon to fulfill His ancient promise to the Patriarchs. If He cannot or will not keep His promise to Abraham, how shall we trust and depend on Him to keep His promise to us? If there is no return of the Jews and no restoration of Jerusalem to it's former Glory, (with the Shekinah Glory there) then how can we believe in an eternal Heaven, and promised eternal life?

3. TO THE JEWS

The interest of the Jews in Jerusalem can be seen in that the city is mentioned over 800 times in the Bible. Jeremiah can best sell us on the special interest which the Jews have for Jerusalem. In chapter 3, verse 17, we read:

> *At that time they shall call Jerusalem the throne of the Lord, and all the nations shall be gathered unto it, to the name of the Lord, to Jerusalem; neither shall they walk any more after the imaginations of the evil heart. In those days the house of Judah shall walk with the house of Israel, and they shall come together out of the land of the north to the land that I have given for an inheritance unto your fathers.*

To endeavor to understand the Jewish attachment to Jerusalem, the Holy Mount and the Holy Land, try to imagine the Christian's hope in Christ without the Resurrection, without eternal life, without Heaven and the New Jerusalem. Without these promises, our hope would be totally shattered. You see, no part of our hope involves any earthly land or kingdom, except possibly the promise that the meek will inherit the earth. Yet to the Jews outside of a new birth in Christ, their only promise is earthly land and an eternal kingdom on earth. Without

Jerusalem and the Mount, and all of the land of promise, the Jewish hope is shattered and the hope that has sustained them for the 2000 years of Diaspora would be gone.

Ever since David chose Jerusalem as the Capital of Israel, nearly 3000 years ago, the Jews have counted Jerusalem very sacred. (See II Samuel 3:10,13,17) 1996 saw the 3000th year celebration of Jerusalem as the capital of Israel. It's sacredness to the State of Israel and the Jewish people is greatly enhanced by the fact that Solomon's Temple was built there. The presence of God's Shekinah Glory on the mercy seat in the Holiest, certainly speaks to them that God has chosen that special place in which to put His name. The book of Zechariah especially prophesied God's choice of Jerusalem again (1:17). All we need to do is go through the book and mark each reference referring to Jerusalem, Zion, the Temple, etc., and we quickly see the significance of these sites to the Jews in the end time.

When we consider the special place which Jerusalem has held in the hearts of the Jews for all of these 3000 years, it certainly pales any claim that the "Palestinians" (whoever they are) have on the city. It is also important to the Jew that their Messiah, our Lord, will again build the Millennial Temple on the site of the earlier Temple (Zechariah 6:12-15).

It is very crucial to the Jew, as well as us Christians,

that God has promised once more to put His name and His glory there, and from there to establish His Son's rule. The raging of the world's nations against Jerusalem is reflective of a world preparing to rise up in resistance to God and his Son as King over all the earth. We see the last day rebellion of the world against God and His Christ clearly described in Psalms 2. The raging nations and Kings of the earth revolt and seek to strip God's control from them. However, God will laugh at their efforts, and will make plain His determination to place King Jesus on His throne in "My Holy Hill Zion" (verse 6). God warns us in these last days, that we are going to find His wrath quite severe upon those who will not honor His control over the Holy Place and His Son's rights to the throne there:

> *Serve the Lord with fear, and rejoice with trembling. Kiss the Son, lest he be angry, and ye perish from the way, when his wrath is kindled but a little. Blessed are they who put their trust in him.*

Jews expect their Messiah to reign from Jerusalem. They also expect their temple to be rebuilt and the glory returned to the sanctuary. Scripture gives them every right to believe these promises. The location of Jerusalem as their capital, and the Temple site are crucial to their hope.

If you are ever privileged to visit Jerusalem, you may have opportunity to be taken below the Temple Mount where there are exploration tunnels excavated under it's foundations. As you proceed northward, you will come to a certain place. [Note: They have now opened the tunnel through to the Via Delorosa near St. Stevens gate.] There you will see a sign against a rock barrier that reads:

"Beyond these stones lies the Holiest of All."

With Sinai in their souls and the memory of the Shekinah still glowing in their hearts, the faithful Jews hold highest respect for the Mount and the special place where the Ark rested. They cannot and will not negotiate it away.

4. TO THE MUSLIMS

It is a fact, as ironic as it may sound, the Muslim faith had no early interest in the Holy Land or the City of Jerusalem except for it being just a small part of the total Arabic world. While Mecca and Madina took on extremely important rolls in Islam, Jerusalem and the land of Israel was left to decay in desolation, important only to wandering Bedouins. Jerusalem by name is never once mentioned in the Koran, and except for a very questionable fantasy taught by later day Muslims, (that Mohammed ascended from there), there is no real or rational proof that the revered prophet ever visited Jerusalem. However, always in mainstream Islam, there has been expressed a disdain for the promises of God to

Isaac and Israel for the land and the city. Every effort has been made by Muslims to resist any hope of Christ's return or the coming of a Jewish Messiah.

When Bible prophecies began literally to be fulfilled, and the wheels of world diplomacy began to be used to put the Jews back in their ancient land as was promised, suddenly the Muslim world became very interested in Jerusalem and the Land of Israel. Using such foolish things as the old anti-Jewish propaganda as the "Protocols of the Learned Elders of Zion" (a document which is widely distributed today among the world of Islam), and an anti-Semitic interpretation of Political Zionism, the Muslim world set out to stir up a whole world against the Jews return and the modern day State of Israel. Now, mostly out of defiance to the Jews, the God of the Jews, and their hope of Messiah, the Muslims worldwide have rallied to make Jerusalem a most important quest of Islam.

Tiny Israel, less in size than the state of Vermont, is not one tenth of one percent of the land mass controlled by Islam, yet to hear the propaganda coming out of terrorist organizations, you would think that Islam rises and falls by their control over Jerusalem. The very existence of Israel and the return of the Jews, is a direct challenge to the basic tenants of Islam, which teaches that there is no other God but Allah, and no other holy people but the Muslims.

In actuality, it is an ancient hate, bred into the soul of the sons of Ishmael and Esau for their having not received the spiritual blessing and covenant of God from the house of Abraham. Joined by the Hagarians (children of Hagar the Egyptian), and the sons of Abraham's later wife Katurah, (after Sarah had died) these nations have perpetuated that ancient hate against the covenant which God made with Isaac and Jacob. It is certainly not that they need the Land of Israel for any economic or social reason. It is just that they do not want God's promises fulfilled to the Jew lest it challenge their particular brand of faith.

5. TO GOD AND TO THE LORD JESUS CHRIST

I think we could not pass up the subject of the importance of Jerusalem to various ones without mentioning it's extreme significance the city holds for God Himself, and for Jesus our Lord. Why, from ancient times, has Jerusalem been chosen by God as the center of His activity on Earth? We may have to wait for explanation when we appear before Him. But no serious student of the Bible, or any one acquainted with the Father, can question it's importance to Him. Over 800 times in the Bible, Jerusalem is mentioned by name. It is alluded to many more times. For reasons known only to God himself, Jerusalem had special significance to him as early as Abraham's day, over 400 years before David made it the capital of Israel. Already, a priest of the Most High God, Melchizedek, reigned there, and it was for ancient reasons that Abraham was directed to Mt. Moriah (the Temple Mount) to sacrifice Isaac.

CHAPTER 4

THE JERUSALEM COVENANT

It seems to us worthy of consideration in any discussion of the Jerusalem problem today, to refer to and expound upon, two subjects relating to a Covenant over Jerusalem. In the crisis situation, it seems rational to assume that there will have to be some kind of "final status" reached concerning Jerusalem which probably will come in the form of an agreement or "covenant." Such an agreement will have to meet the satisfaction of all of the great monotheistic religions (i.e. Muslim, Christian, and Jew) as well as some kind of international control, which also would serve to conciliate all of the world's interests in the region. The making of such an arrangement has been at the heart of all the peace initiatives in the past. None to this point have met the extreme demands, which stand at such great odds between the interested parties.

To understand the Biblical prophecy concerning just such a treaty, we will need to refer to the passage of Scripture, which has been the focal point of eschatological expositors for the past centuries, especially since the turn of the 20th century. That text can be found in Deuteronomy 9:24-27. From this text in comparison with other references which complement this text, scholars have concluded that:

1. During the last seven years before the Lord's return, there would be a Covenant made concerning the Holy Land.

2. That the covenant would especially concern Jerusalem and the Temple Mount.

3. That it would involve the Antichrist, inasmuch as the breaking of it would bring the "Abomination of Desolation" referred to by Jesus (Matthew 24:15).

4. The general consensus has been that the breaking of the Covenant and the Abomination of Desolation would be accomplished when the Beast sets himself up in the Holy Place and proclaimed that he is God (I1 Thessalonians 2:4).

5. That the breaking of this covenant would also

perpetrate the Jews of Judea (i.e. the West Bank), to have to flee.

6. That it would be this breaking of the Covenant and the necessity of the Jews to flee and the setting up of the Antichrist in Jerusalem that would precipitate the final battle.

With all of the world's attention upon Jerusalem, and the volatile situation there, it seems imperative that such an agreement be made very soon. That's why any prophecy concerning such a Covenant becomes extremely interesting and exciting. Let us refer to that text under consideration.

DANIEL'S SEVENTY WEEK COVENANT

We are told by the prophet Daniel, (in his famous 70 week prophecy) recorded in the 9th chapter of Daniel. that there would come a seven year Covenant, confirmed by the world, in the last years of this age. The angel showed Daniel what would befall his people, the city of Jerusalem and the Temple Mount in the future. Starting in Daniel's day with the edict from the Persian King, allowing the foundations of the Temple to be laid, there was to be 490 years of future history concerning Israel and Jerusalem. At the end of 69 cycles of 7 years (or 483 years), the Messiah would be cut off, the city destroyed and until the end, wars and desolations of the city and the land were determined. This all happened exactly on time as Daniel was shown. The Lord's crucifixion took place exactly 483 years after the Edict of Darias the Mede to rebuild the Temple. From that time, the Jews relationship to the City of Jerusalem as the capital of the State of Israel would be cut off, the Church age would be grafted in, and the time clock of Daniels 70 week prophecy would be stopped. The *"times of the Gentiles,"* and their trodding down of Jerusalem, (Luke 21:24), would begin and would continue until the Jews return. The prophetic time clock of this prophecy would start again with the "confirming" of a seven year covenant over Jerusalem and the Temple Mount (Daniel 9:27).

At the end, 7 more years were to take place. These years were to start with the affirmation of a Covenant over Jerusalem and the Temple Mount. Its confirmation would highlight the final end, in which several things would be accomplished. (Please refer to Daniel 9:20-27.)

1. Bring an end to sin and transgression.
2. Fulfill all visions and prophecies.
3. Make reconciliation for iniquity.
4. Bring in everlasting righteousness.
5. End Gentile occupation of Jerusalem.
6. Anoint the most Holy.

According to what the Angel told Daniel, this Covenant would allow the Jews to rebuild again the Temple and begin animal sacrifices. However, the Covenant would be broken, as we have shown above, in the middle of the 7-year period, (i.e. 31/2 years) and the Abomination of Desolation set up. Some have taught that the prophecy was fulfilled in Antiochus Epiphany's time when the sacrilegious Greek ruler sacrificed a pig on the altar of the Temple and set up an image of a Greek God in the sanctuary. But Jesus himself spoke of this Abomination as being in the future of His day (Matthew 24:15).

We understand this to be the abomination accomplished when the Devil, (incarnate in a man) sets himself upon the throne in Jerusalem (I1 Thessalonians 2:4). Jesus said it was to come and would cause the righteous Jews to flee (Matthew 24:15,16). Daniel 11:22-32 gives the details. In verses 22 and 23 a league is made, but deceit is at work. The Jews will at first trust him and believe him to be the Messiah. He gains world recognition by his campaigns, but verse 28 reveals the beginning of his indignation toward the Covenant.

According to the Angel the Covenant was to be "confirmed." *The Amplified Bible* states it thus: "And he shall enter into a strong and firm Covenant." *Strong's Concordance* shows the Hebrew word to be "Gabar," which means, "to strengthen." The translators into English must have understood it to mean to strengthen an already existent Covenant, for the English word "confirm" certainly corroborates that thought. It means to approve, attest, ratify, uphold, support, and strengthen what is already understood. This, of course, suggests that some form of a former Covenant had already been established, and would be affirmed at the beginning of a 7-year period.

I would like to suggest that it is altogether possible that a form of the Covenant has already been made. Possibly what might be called the first draft of such a Covenant. Let's look for a moment at the background for the development of just such a Covenant at this present time.

YASSAR ARAFAT AND OSLO

At Oslo, in September of 1993, The Rabin/Perez team drafted what became known as the "Oslo Accords" or "Declaration of Principles." No more than the time it took for the ink to dry, did this "Great Leap" begin to be the Great Flop, and the Document began to gather dust. When it began to be evident to the State of Israel, and particularly to the Jews, that Rabin and Perez were intent on compromising Jerusalem and the Temple Mount by bowing to Mr. Clinton and international pressure, a signal of concern began to be raised. Disquieted and even perturbed, Jews worldwide could see their ancient dreams being shattered. They saw a bloody revolutionary, who had been shown for what he was, and who had been defeated and driven out of the Mid-East in the Lebanon campaign, pulled back out of exile and put back in power. If Mr. Clinton had been wise and not caught up with his own importance and agenda, he would have left Arafat out of it. Now the United States and Israel are up to their ears in terror and revolution, all created and promoted by this "terrorist."

The resurrection of Yassar Arafat, the "Grand Master of International Terrorism and Israel's arch-enemy" (Yesha Report, October '93), gave him new and heightened respectability. Both Mr. Clinton and the Rabin/Perez team hoped that he would reign in the Hamas, and other fundamental terrorists of the PLO sympathizers.

This is the same sort of diplomatic nonsense that caused our support of Saddam Hussein in his campaign against Iran; and that set up Castro in Cuba with State Department support. It is shear folly to support these wicked dictators on any level for any cause. It is time these do-gooders wake up to understand that terrorists and dictators will never change and will use every advantage to further their own power and end.

On September 13, 1993 (just 2300 days before the end of the century) Yasser Arafat and Yitzak Rabin made an illegitimate and ill-fated agreement. Arafat is not a Palestinian. He was born in Egypt. He only came to the West Bank after being trained in the Soviet Union in the trade of Terror. He and his family came only after the State of Israel began to build a society out of the chaos, which had been left by the Muslims upon the land for centuries. Arafat would never have been anything except for two factors: one, the Western Media, looking for any support for their anti-Israel stance- hoped he would be a leader for the "Palestinian cause." It seems to us so ludicrous that they could not see the disdain for him even among the Muslim States. When he was run out of Lebanon and needed a place to retreat, he could not find one Muslim Nation which would allow him in. Jordan had already run him out. That's how he came to be in Lebanon. All the rest knew him for what he was. Two, the Israeli/Palestinian conflict was the ideal political upheaval that all revolutionaries use to foster revolt worldwide. But no matter, revolutions world wide for 50 years have had the mainstream media's sentiment and support. He simply took advantage of the vacuum left when Jordan, after taking the West Bank from Israel, and brought the Marxist Revolution to the Middle East with the purpose of overthrowing the democratic State of Israel. The "Palestinians" as a people do not now and never have existed. They are totally an Arafat invention.

His cousin, Multi Hag Amin al Husseine, was Mufti of Jerusalem when he joined the German cause with Hitler. It was also a revelation to me while I was with the troops in Lebanon, to discover that Arafat's own brother was head of the "Red Crescent," a Marxist-leaning News Source from which all of our major Media was receiving their information for reporting on the Lebanon war. This certainly accounts for why the reports to the American people were so biased and untrue. Falsified information in favor of Arafat and against Israel was so contrary to what 53 other Americans and I were actually observing in the field. It also conveniently ignored the evidence of devastation and carnage which Arafat and his cutthroats had worked against the people of Southern Lebanon.

Mr. Rabin carried the respect of most of Israel until the Oslo Accords. From that time on, only the secular part of Israel continued support. The Jewish community began to hold him in deep suspect. He was a solid supporter of National Zionism and the right of the Jewish State to exist, but he had neither leaning toward the religious purpose of the State, nor any Biblical relationship to the Modern State of Israel. In fact, three days before his death, he pounded on the Knesset podium and yelled, "We do not believe in greater Israel, we do not believe in the Bible promise." Three days later a Jew killed him. I personally believe that Mr. Rabin was quite frustrated by the pressure being put on him by the Media and Mr. Clinton. You could certainly see the consternation on his face when, on the White House Lawn and in front of Bill Clinton and the World, he was forced to shake hands with the archenemy of Israel, Yassar Arafat.

Mr. Perez has always been deeply committed to a Marxist style of socialism. He served as Vice chairman of

Socialist International and made "Dos Capital" his major reading material. He made the boast privately that, if he was elected Prime Minister of Israel, he would immediately move to Internationalize Jerusalem and turn it to the Pope of Rome to administrate. David Hunt, in his book "Cup of Trembling" quoted a letter which Mr. Perez was said to have sent to the Pope stating those very intentions.

In the Rabin/Perez sell-out, Israel was to withdraw from Gaza, Jericho, and Bethlehem. Withdrawal was to be complete by April of 1994. Palestinians were to elect a government, which would take over from Israel on about 90% of the West Bank. By the spring of 1996 final status talks concerning Jerusalem and the Temple Mount and the return of refugees to the West Bank, along with settlement over the settlers of the West Bank, was to come to the table. Israel was to return to the pre-1967 borders. In the end there was to be a Palestinian State. 50% of the land to be handed over was Israeli owned.

A Palestinian Council was to control the land and resources of the 144 Jewish communities, and all Jews were to get out of Gaza, Hebron, Bethlehem, and Jericho. This would leave a completely indefensible situation for Israel. It would cut the nation in two at its mid-section, leaving only a 11-mile wide border. It would place all Israel in range of terrorist and Katyusha rockets, and all of the Palestinian positions would be on high ground overlooking the cities and towns, highways, and all of the industry and infrastructure of Israel.

Immediately upon the signing of the Accords in 1993, Arabs began to march in victory parades and shout, "slaughter the Jews," and "with blood and fire we will redeem Palestine" (all of Israel). Other slogans were "Gaza first, then Jericho, then Jerusalem" and "welcome to greater Palestine." Finally Israeli citizens began to see the picture. A reaction among Israeli people rippled through the nation with the slogan "Rabin has no mandate to negotiate with the PLO." Around the clock demonstrations flooded Tel Aviv. In Jerusalem, massive rallies of 250,000 and more took place on Sept. 6th, a week before the signing at Oslo. Of course the agreements died almost as soon as they were signed. The only life they had was maintained by media life support, but it was terminal from birth. No part of the agreement was kept by the Palestinians, therefore Israel, after withdrawing form Bethlehem and Jericho, found themselves in nothing but further terror and stopped the withdrawal. No Permanent Status talks took place in 1996, and all is still in limbo today.

The Peace Treaty negotiations were forced upon Israel by what could be said to be extortion, or even a little white blackmail. President Bush Sr. refused to allow a loan guarantee of one billion dollars to Israel. The loan was needed to help house and establish 250,000 Russian immigrants that were flooding Israel at the time. They were not asking for a handout nor even a grant. Israel simply asked for a guarantee. Remember, Israel is the only nation in the world who has faithfully paid back every loan made to it by the United States.

COULD OSLO HAVE BEEN THE COVENANT OF DANIEL?

The nature and content of this "Covenant" or more perfectly Peace Treaty, is worthy of some discussion. Is it possible that this covenant for the land, is actually the covenant spoken of in Daniel 9:27? To us it is very doubtful, although the Oslo Accord was given a 7-year period for completion.

It is more likely that the newly "confirmed" Jerusalem Covenant, which we have mentioned and will enlarge upon later is at least a forerunner of the covenant.

Could it be that the Jerusalem Covenat might be an extension of The Holy Covenant of God, made with Abraham? Could it be that in some revival of interest by the World Community, diplomats of Europe, America, and even Asia would finally be forced to recognize God's plan and right to the land? Could the Orthodox Jewish Faithful finally prevail, and gain access to the Temple? Could this covenant actually recognize the Jews right to the city of Jerusalem as the capital of Israel? Such a contingency would surely necessitate the intervention of God in a most unusual way in order to convince an agnostic world to such an arrangement. We think however, just such a surprising eventuality is entirely possible, and we will project our reasons later.

It is possible, however, that the covenant of agreement would be more in the form of a compromise among the warring faction. Even at present, and in reference to former resolutions of the Security Council of the United Nations, America, Europe, and even within the Arab and Jewish communities, those diplomats are circulating strong suggestions to internationalize Jerusalem. As early as when Henry Kissinger was Secretary of State under Ronald Reagan, Mr. Kissinger suggested that Jerusalem be internationalized and the Temple Mount be compromised among the various interested religions. Ehud Olmart, previous Mayor of Jerusalem, seems to feel that the Temple Mount be declared God's property therefore belonging to no certain state or people. An administration committee involving all of the interested parties would be set up, not to claim any ownership but simply to deal with the day-to-day operations of the Mount. There are strong prophecies which seem to support just such an agreement. There may be a compromise between the two above scenarios, and of course other possibilities, which have not yet presented themselves. Either of the above certainly makes room for international involvement which can and will set up the final stage for the Antichrist's appearance on the scene.

It is our persuasion, however, that the Covenant spoken of in Daniel 9:27 will not be a Peace Treaty, although it will certainly contain elements of a temporary peace, but will in fact be a sacred pledge by the Jewish Faithful toward Jerusalem and the Temple Mount. We will share the reasons for our convictions later on in this writing.

Regardless of the final scenario, The Antichrist will set himself up as God in the Temple of God in Jerusalem. Verse 31 speaks of his pollution of the Sanctuary, (by his throne being there) and verse 32 tells of his wickedness against the Sacrifices and the Covenant. All of this must presuppose an arrangement, which will allow the Jews to build some kind of sanctuary on the Temple Mount.

He will corrupt many of the Jews by flatteries, thereby gaining at least temporary support of some part of the Jewish community. More than likely it would be the secular side of Jewry. However, evidently many of the faithful will see through his deceptions and will flee his kingdom, to be cared for in Petra (vs. 33-35). He will come to his end, and none will help him (v. 45).

It will all end with a "flood" of armies in the Middle East. All of this is set up by the making of a Covenant over Jerusalem. It is altogether possible that the very Covenant being sought today by both the World Community and the Jewish people is in fact that very Covenant spoken of by Daniel.

THE JERUSALEM COVENANT

With all of the world's interest in Jerusalem, and at the time when it seemed Jerusalem and the World Community rendered the Temple Mount most susceptible to compromise, the Jewish Sanhedrin worldwide made it's statement loud and clear. It was just prior to the Oslo Accords, which would take place in September of 1993. The Jews worldwide realized that powerful world factions were near an agreement which would divide the Holy Land and the City of Jerusalem, and compromise the Temple Mount.

So as we have earlier revealed, on Jerusalem Day in May 1992, a Covenant, known as the JERUSALEM COVENANT, was circulated among the heavies of Israel and the Jewish leadership in Jerusalem for their signature. It has been signed by most of the leaders of the Israeli Government as well as the leading Rabbis of Israel. It was then being circulated among world Jewry and was put in force at a great Jerusalem Day celebration commemorating the 3000th anniversary of Jerusalem as the Capital of the State of Israel. That celebration was held in May of 1996. Interestingly enough, that is the very same date that Jerusalem was to come up again for negotiations in the Peace Agreement between Israel and the PLO. It is also worthy to note that those promoting the Jerusalem Covenant are the Torah Faithful, who await the coming Messiah to re-establish Israel and build the Temple. They claim that it is the Lord who will build up Jerusalem (Psalm 147:2 and Zechariah 6:12). Therefore these do not even recognize the State of Israel today.

The Jerusalem Covenant was not highly publicized nor brought to public notice at the time. The reason for this lack will be seen as we discuss the contents of the covenant and it's highly explosive declarations.

COVENANT IS IN STATE NEXT TO THE DECLARATION OF INDEPENDENCE

I had heard some mention of the covenant, but found it quite hard to trace down and document. While I was in Tel Aviv in 1995, I was able to get on it's trail and found a publisher who had actually published the document in several languages. It had been published of course in its original Hebrew form. It was also published in English as well as a number of other languages. I rushed over to the publishers and obtained several copies of it.

In the fall of 1996, just months after the document had finally been presented for confirmation, I very much desired to see the actual original copy. I had heard that it was on display in the Knesset building in Jerusalem. Taking a leave on an off-day from the tour I was hosting, I asked the Guide to take me by the Parliament Building. Since security was extremely high at that time, I was not sure I would be allowed into the building, let alone the privilege of viewing the document.

Taking only a couple of ministers with me, I approached the Knesset. We were allowed through the gate and into the building and were taken to the Chief of Security. When I stated my request, surprise overtook him and thus the beginning of an interesting experience. He immediately asked if I was a Jew. When I told him that I was not, he was very moved. He asked how I knew about the Covenant. I explained that I kept up on all of the events concerning Bible Prophecy- from the Jewish prophets, which concerned the latter day return of the Jews, and the establishment of the State of Israel. He again asked me if I were not a Jew. Then he said: "You are a Gentile and you are interested? I will allow you to view the document even though I am not supposed to even allow you on the second floor. You wait here."

Momentarily he returned and ushered us to the second floor, where, to our surprise and delight, was the official signed document entitled: "Jerusalem Covenant." To add to the sense of special importance which the document held, we found it on display in the same case and along side the Declaration of Independence of the State of Israel.

As we stood in awe, viewing the documents together, I was nearly overcome with emotion. Tears filled my eyes as I tried to comprehend the tremendous significance, which I believed these documents portrayed. There it lay in State as we had suspected, encased in the same display as the Declaration of Independence, which certainly demonstrated its imposing weight to the people and the nation. It was, of course, written in Hebrew, but I had in my hand a copy translated into English.

I took note and pointed out the signatures at the bottom. There was the signature of the President of the State of Israel, President of the Supreme Court of Israel, as well as the signatures of the Prime Minister, and Deputy Prime Minister, the Speaker of the Knesset, the Chief Rabbis of both the Sephardi and Ashkenazi, Chairman of the World Zionist Congress, the head of the Department. Of Jerusalem Affairs, and the Mayor of Jerusalem.

A period of silence prevailed, and after some moments to gain my composure, I began to explain to my minister brethren the background of this document, and why I felt it so important to both the State of Israel, the Jews world-wide and also those of us who studied the Jewish prophets. I looked over at the Chief Security officer who stood opposite us on the far side of the display. He was crying big tears, which dripped off his chin. When I looked his way it must have invited him to break the silence.

"How do you know these things." he asked? I explained, "from my study of the Jewish prophets."

In total amazement he asked again if I was not a Jew. I felt that I should impress him more this time that I was not a Jew. I said to him: "Sir, I am not a Jew. I am just an old pig-eating Gentile which has been adopted into the heritage of Israel by faith." He asked, "If you are not a Jew, why are you so moved?" Again, I tried to explain to him how the Jewish prophets might have prophesied this very document. I also explained that many other prophecy teachers among the Gentile Evangelical Churches of America had been expecting a Covenant for years.

He was very overcome to find that Gentiles might be so interested in the survival of the State of Israel and so interested in Jerusalem as the State's Capital. As we continued to discuss these things, he showed every evidence of delight and surprise, and he cried all the way through our conversation with him. That outsiders could care so much for his beloved city and Temple was most welcome. He confessed his own love and commitment for the city, almost as if to confirm his agreement with the document before us.

You can see by this story how deeply the State of Israel as a whole, and the Jewish community both in Israel and worldwide, feel about the city of Jerusalem and the Temple Mount. It was probably one of the most exciting and memorable experiences among my score or more of trips to the Holy Land.

I relate this story first of all to confirm the actual existence of the document that I shall discuss, and also to impress the reader of it's very special importance, even though it has gone almost completely unnoticed by the World Community and media. And there are reasons.

First, the Jews themselves, not willing to stir up any more anti-Israel sentiment would just as soon it be kept an internal matter. Second, the International Community does not care to be involved with its highly explosive text. Of course, the Muslim community does not take it seriously, assured that it cannot be meaningful in the present situation. Third, the media, not willing to show any semblance of a pro-Israel stance, has not recognized the Covenant's validity, therefore has not reported it.

CONTROVERSY OF ZION

Because this document is so controversial, let's spend a little time on the background of the dispute. It is, in fact an age-old dispute. The controversy over Jerusalem and the Temple Mount has perpetrated numerous wars and confrontations in the Middle East through the centuries.

The controversy actually can be traced as far back as the Assyrians, and Babylonians, who thought it necessary to subdue Israel. Evidently the Temple posed some real or imaginary threat to the hegemony of the Empires. Persia, after subduing Babylon had kings who felt that religious freedom was important to pulling the Empire together and therefore were disposed to allow Ezra and Nehemiah to rebuild the City of Jerusalem and the Temple. However, great controversy arose in the Empire making it necessary for the Jews to build "in troublous times." The City became a covenanted place for the Greeks who fought many battles there.

Antiochus set up a palace there and polluted the Temple so seriously that some thought it the "Abomination of Desolation" spoken of by Daniel. These Desolations brought on the Hesomonian revolt. For a short time, Israel was relatively free of Imperial dominance, but soon the Romans came to power. Rome disdained the Jews and their monotheism, and out of distrust placed the Idumean Herods over them. It seemed to the Jews that the controversy of Zion was settled, as life under the Idumean Kings seemed to be acceptable. Herod greatly expanded the Temple Grounds and beautified the Temple itself. But Jesus foresaw and foretold the soon-coming destruction of the Temple and the City (Luke 21:24, Matthew 24:1). In AD 70, Titus and Vespasian totally destroyed Jerusalem and the Temple. Since that time "wars and desolations" have been "determined" as spoken of by Daniel (Daniel 9:26). Only the Western Wall of the Temple remained and that portion of the Temple complex is known as the Wailing Wall, or the Western Wall, today.

Four great Empires fought over it's control. In the Middle Ages came the Crusades, Salidin, Byzantium, Suliemen and the Ottoman Empire. Finally the Jews to their Ancient City and Temple Mount have enhanced the problem in our day by the formulation of the State of Israel, and the renewed claim. For centuries no one paid any major attention to the city nor the Mount. Desolation and ruin were its state, and had been specifically prophesied. When the Jews were allowed by UN mandate to re-establish the State of Israel in 1948, suddenly the whole Muslim world rose up and made claim to the City.

There are two points of focal interest today. One, It is clearly prophesied that the final controversy of the world will rest here, and the final battle of the ages will be fought over it. Two, It cannot be argued either that the predictions of those preaching and teaching Bible prophecy were extremely accurate. Today, the focus of the whole world is on Jerusalem. It is the catalyst for terrorist and extremists and has become the major hindrance to world peace today.

Without any consideration of Bible Prophecy, it is obvious that there will of necessity have to come some kind of an agreement or treaty, which will address the Jerusalem problem to the satisfaction of the Jews, Christians, Muslims, and the International Community of Nations.

Gentile powers were forced to take control of the Holy Land and the City of Jerusalem after the First World War. Allied forces led by Britain brought down the Ottoman Turk Empire and received mandate over Palestine. Hoping to settle the whole Arab world, and also accommodate the Jews after the holocaust in Europe, new lines and boundaries were drawn and governments were put in place. Israel was mandated their ancient home land with hopes that world peace could now be fact. Immediately seven surrounding nations attacked the tiny Nation of Israel. Israel won and retained her borders all but to the East where they lost the West Bank to Jordan. Jordan soon disclaimed the West Bank but retained control over the Temple Mount. It is of prime interest to note that the Muslims accepted all the borders drawn up by allied forces except the borders of Israel.

Suddenly, the controversy of Zion raged again, this time raising the tempest to world proportions. A great awakening of the Muslim nations arose. Although not one mention of Jerusalem can be found in the Quran. It seemed of little interest to Mohammed. Now the controversy of Zion has accelerated to such a pitch that Jerusalem, true to Bible Prophecy, has become "a cup of trembling to all nations round about" (Zechariah 12:2) and a "burdensome stone for all people"(all nations) (ibid. verse 3).

At the present time and during negotiations for the past 55 years, Jerusalem has been a subject no one dares touch. In all of the late "Peace Treaties" it has always been relegated to "final status" talks at some future time. A "final solution" status seems to be the only way to get any agreement at all. We think however, that no agreement will ever be worth its paper until the status of Jerusalem is decided. Even the UN has not dared to tackle the controversy of Zion.

Early on in the 1948-50 Resolutions, it was relegated to be an International City, with a very interesting and special status. It was called "Corpus Septrum" (a separate body). They decided that the "whole world was one body, and Jerusalem another." A separate city from all nations, it was to be an International City. Although this has been the official status of Jerusalem for nearly five decades, the World Order has not dared push its demand upon Israel to give up its control of Jerusalem as its capital.

The controversy is further enhanced now by the prospects and demands of the "Palestinians" who claim it as their inherited capital. They claim, either that the Jews have been so long time gone, and since then the Muslim faith has controlled it for over 1000 years, that it is now theirs (Ezekiel 11:14-19). Or, that the State of Israel never did exist in the first place and there never has been a Jewish Temple.

The controversy is heightened when we see that the Jewish State and the Jewish faith have at it's epicenter, the sacred history and possession of the City and the Mount. To abandon it would be equal to Islam abandoning Mecca, or Christianity the New Jerusalem, which in either case would be paramount to their faith and existence. So firm is Jewish faith established as relating to the Mount that it goes clear back to Abraham who would have sacrificed Isaac there, but for the promise of another sacrifice which "in this Mount you will see it." At the dedication of the Temple of Solomon (2 Chronicles 7) God accepted it and placed his name there forever.

No Jew could ever be known as the one who gave away Jerusalem. It would be sheer Anathema. By the same token, no Muslim could ever be known as the one to give up Jerusalem. It would be his Anathema. Because of the hundreds of sacred sights in Jerusalem, to the whole Christian world, including the Catholics and Orthodox each with fast holdings, the Russian and Armeanian churches, not to leave out the fast interest and holdings of the Coptic, Morite, and Evangelical Christian people, adding to this the world interest in ancient antiquities - you have a time bomb with a short fuse.

The controversy of Zion rages. It is a "seething cal-dron" among the nations. It is the only initiate in the world which has the potential of worldwide holocaust, and bringing the whole western world to its knees. What is soon to come over the controversy of Zion can only be described in apocalyptic expression.

This background is given in an effort to establish the importance to the world of a final status over Jerusalem. No world peace can be a reality without settling the age-old controversy of Zion. Startling scriptures can be found which refer to the final status, and the West Bank problem of *"dividing the Land."* As Jordan of today, (Mt. Sier of the past) tries to possess the "ancient high places of the West Bank, or the "Mountains of Israel" (Ezekiel chapters 35 and 36), they are soon to discover that *"the Lord was there"*(v. 10). A world must soon come to the conclusion, whether they agree or not, that the Great God of Israel has much to say about the final status. As this controversy came to a head again at the Oslo Accord, Jews worldwide felt a necessity to state very clearly their commitment to Jerusalem and the Temple Mount.

AFFIRMATION OF THE COVENANT OF JERUSALEM

First, the date of its affirmation is important. We must mention that it has already been "confirmed" by the State of Israel and the Jews worldwide, but just such a document (if not this one) must be confirmed by the world community some time soon. It's affirmation came on the 3000th celebration of David's declaration of Jerusalem to be the capital of the State of Israel. David moved his capital from Hebron to the Jebusite City, hereafter to be known as Zion. It's signing came just 2300 days from the turn of the century. The Covenant was meant to be a clear statement in the face of Oslo. It clearly affirmed that the Jews had no intention of backing away from Jerusalem as the "Capital of the State of Israel, undivided and whole." It was clearly and decisively a counter offensive to the give-away arranged by the

Rabin/Perez agreement with the Palestinians. It was
meant to fly in the face of Palestinian claims that had sur-
faced from the office of Yassar Arafat purporting that
there was no historical evidence of Jewish presence in
Jerusalem, nor a Jewish Temple on the Mount. Thus
(according to Arafat) the Jews had no prior claim to the
Holy City. In the face of such utter foolishness, the Jews
made clear that their claim was a blood libel. If we observe
the affirmations in the statements of the Covenant, we
cannot doubt the depth of its meaning, nor can we doubt
its absolute clarity of purpose in relationship to the people and the city.

STATEMENTS OF THE COVENANT

Let's look at some of the declarations of the Jerusalem
Covenant. The whole of the text will be printed in adden-
dum to this writing.

The Covenant first set the date in the Jewish year of
5752, just 25 years after the Six Day War of 1967. One not
well versed in these matters might wonder why the Six Day
War should be mentioned. It was during that war, on June
6th of 1967, that Jerusalem was retaken from Jordan, and
the date that marks the Jewish control of Jerusalem for the
first time since it was lost to the Romans in AD 70. That
date was just 1922 years after the Temple's destruction by
Titus and the 10th Army. It was also 12 years after the
Knesset had declared Jerusalem "united and whole, the

Capital of the State of Israel." The document then confirmed the gathering together of the "sovereign national
officials, and leaders of our communities everywhere." So
it became a clear statement that:

"Jerusalem, united and whole, is the Capital of the
State of Israel."

And again, at the end:

"We shall bind you to us forever---We love you, Oh
Jerusalem, with eternal love, with unbounded love,
we have been martyred for you, we have yearned
for you."

After the introduction above there followed a Bible
verse from Psalm 122:2:

Our feet stand within your gates O Jerusalem.

Now note this statement:

"We have returned to the place where the Lord
vowed to the descendants of Abraham, father of our
Nation, to the City of David, King of Israel, where
Solomon, son of David built the Holy Temple, and
to the Capital City, where a second Temple was
erected in the days of Ezra and Nehemiah."

It then states the original purpose:

"..establishing the places holy to the people of all

religions shall be protected from any discretion of free access."

Finally, it affirms:

"We enter into this Covenant. We shall bind you (Jerusalem) to us forever; we shall bind you to us in faithfulness, with righteousness and justice. With steadfast love and compassion. We love You, O Jerusalem, with eternal love; With unbounded love...We have been martyred for you. We have yearned for you; we have clung to you; forevermore our home shall be within you." "In certification of this covenant we sign."

These are strong words in the face of the present negotiations, and against the backdrop of Arafat's absolute demands that Jerusalem be the Capital of the State of Palestine. It is the cry of the prayers at the Western Wall, "Come Messiah, come Messiah, come Messiah." The Jews may have been blinded in part, but there is one thing they have not missed, and that is the hope of the coming Messiah. They know that Satan will be rebuked and Jerusalem will be chosen (Zechariah 1:17, and 3:2). They know that many nations will flow into Jerusalem, according to Zechariah 8. Here we have a prophecy of the great tourist industry that now flourishes in Israel. Zechariah 2:10-13 clearly preaches their hope also:

Sing and rejoice, o daughter of Zion; for, lo, I come, and I will dwell in the midst of thee, saith the Lord. And many nations shall be joined to the Lord in that day, and shall be my people; and I will dwell in the midst of thee, and thou shalt know that the Lord of hosts hath sent me unto thee. And the Lord shall inherit Judah, (West Bank), his portion in the Holy Land, and shall choose Jerusalem again.

A COVENANT NOT A PEACE TREATY

It is important that we observe the exact language and setting of prophecy (Daniel 9:20-27) which speaks of the coming Covenant. Daniel was not told that this Covenant would have anything to do with peace treaties, although we may assume there is a relationship. The point is it probably is not a Peace Treaty per se.

Since the whole subject of the 70 weeks prophecy concerns *"thy people and thy holy city,"* (Daniel 9:24), Daniel had been praying about *"thy city Jerusalem thy holy mountain"* (v.16) *"the sanctuary that is desolate"* (v.17) and *"the city called by thy name"* (v.18), etc. It was while he was praying thus (v.20), that the angel came to inform him what was *"determined upon thy people and upon thy holy city"*(v.24). So we see that the subject of the prophecy is the city of Jerusalem as it relates to the Jews. One of the main subjects is the final end of the occupation of Jerusalem by Gentile nations, and the final anointing of the Most Holy to rule from there.

We see that the covenant is not directly concerned with "peace" in the Holy Land. It does not address the

Palestinian/Jewish problem of dividing the land. It's subject is Jerusalem and the people of Israel. It is not called a treaty nor an agreement, which would have made use of the Hebrew word "chozeh, or chozuth." The Angel might even have used the Hebrew word "mesharim," (translated "agreement") later in Daniel (11:6).

A treaty is thought of more in a political or diplomatic form of negotiation. It usually has little or no spiritual or eternal connotations. It is a negotiated arrangement between two parties of equal obligation. A give and take or tit for tat until some ground of equality is reached. It is our persuasion by the words used that the Covenant spoken of here is far deeper, and of more eternal impact than simply a "mesharim," or "chozeh." In the Biblical context here, another word is used.

However the word translated "covenant" that the Angel used is the Hebrew word "berith." This is a word used over 250 times and always represents an arrangement or contract mainly concerning spiritual matters. The root meaning here is "a cutting," therefore a blood issue or "contract in blood." For instance the sacrificial covenant for our salvation, is more than a treaty. Certainly, there is no negotiations on our part. Man is never in a position to bargain with God on any matter, let alone his salvation. There is no negotiation to it, nor is there any position of neutrality or equality. We must rely completely and totally on God's promise. His mercy and grace are our only grounds.

By the "cutting" of sacrifice, (the spilling of blood), God means to demonstrate the seriousness and surety of His promise. Note again, it is totally on God's part that the promise is made. We simply express our faith and acceptance of the covenant by obedience to him. This "blood covenant" started clear back in Eden. There blood was let to sacrifice lambs for the skins to cover Adam and Eve's sin. It continued through Abel's sacrifice, also Noah and Abraham. God covenanted with Abraham by instructing him to kill and cut the sacrifices in pieces and lay them out. The presence of God passed between the parts as a demonstration of God's acceptance of the promise to Abraham concerning the Land, the City and the Holy Mount (Genesis 25). You see Abraham had no part in the promise - just to accept it by faith. No negotiations took place. There was no equality, or bargaining. God, by his own sovereign grace and election, chose Abraham and his seed for His own purpose.

The same positions of God and man are seen in the promise of the rainbow of Noah. It was God's covenant assurance and promise that there would never be another worldwide flood. The Sabbath was another one of God's many covenants with man. Biblically then, a covenant is basically unconditional on man's part and represents a promise from God (see Galatians 3:15).

Another point we think is worth considering. A

covenant calls on God as the sole witness and seldom ever a pact between tribes or nations or individual peoples. The word "berith" is often used in conjunction with other adjectives, such as "Aheb brit" or "brit hesedim" (Covenant Love), "brit tobe" (Covenant goodness), or brit Selam"(Covenant Peace). The Hasidim of the Jews represents those of God's Covenant of Everlasting Love.

Let us not belabor the point further as this could be the subject of a whole separate study. We simply seek to show that a covenant is a far deeper and meaningful arrangement than a treaty. The covenant of Daniel 9:27 which will be confirmed by the Antichrist for a short period of peace will be only an agreement to him and the world, but to the Jews, it will be a covenant of death, a blood cutting, as it were, one that will be honored and kept even at the cost of their lives.

Since, as we have shown, the Covenant came while Daniel was praying for the future of his people in relationship to the City of Jerusalem, and the Land of Israel, it must of necessity be a Covenant concerning these very things. It was to come at the end of a long period of "wars and desolations" and at the time of "the consummation." Therefore it has to come at the final end.

At the end, in the final 7 years, this Covenant is to be "confirmed. If it was to be "confirmed" it would have to be pre-existent as a document already in force. So some pre-existing document must already be in place by some who have that position and authority (verses 25-42). The Antichrist may confirm a treaty and/or agreement, however the "Covenant" is part of a blood oath made earlier. As God often spoke through his prophets, He is confirming his Covenant with Abraham, by returning the Jews back to the land and city in these last days. God promised at that time to remember his Covenant with Abraham and give back the land and city to His posterity.

Since it is not called the *"Holy Covenant"* as spoken of in Daniel 11:30, it probably is not speaking of that particular covenant between God and Abraham, but certainly could be related to it in the sense that it deals with the promises concerning the Land, the City and the Mount.

The Antichrist will break whatever agreement he may have made. Evidently he will also disannul the Covenant and cause the sacrifice to cease. But praise God, he cannot and will not be able to break the Holy Covenant of God with either the Jews nor with us, the Church. He may cause the sacrifices to cease, but he cannot thwart the eternal sacrifice already made on Calvary, and the eternal promise of life made to us by God in that "blood letting." Although to the Jew, the Temple sacrifice would be of prime importance, to us Christ has become the *"mediator of a better covenant, which was established upon better promises"* (Hebrews 8:6). He is the surety of a better Testament, ie. Covenant (Hebrews 7:22). *"Therefore He is able to save them to the uttermost that come unto God by him"* (v. 25). Our Lord was offered as a *"better sacrifice"* (9:23), to *"bear the sins of many"* (9:28). By the time the sacrifices are no longer allowed by the Antichrist, the Lord will soon come in power. Then also these precious people of Abraham will know that His blood, not the blood of bulls and goats (9:14) was shed to forgive their sins. They will mourn for him (Revelation 1:8) and say *"what are these wounds in your hands"* (Zechariah 13:4)? Then *"all Israel shall be saved"* (Romans 11:26).

The Covenant of Daniel, chapter 9, and it's relationship to some sort of peace agreement may be reflected in the mention of the *"prince of the Covenant,* (Daniel 11:22) possibly the Antichrist or a forerunner who negotiates a Covenant. Here it is in the context of a peacemaker (vs. 21 and 24). It is probably then, a part of a peace agreement, which deals mostly with the Jews right to the city of Jerusalem and the Temple Mount. We are told that the *"prince of the covenant"* will be set against the Covenant.(vs.22-32). Here we see that the Covenant had to do with the Holy Covenant." The Holy Covenant harks back to some sacred promise of record. This can only be God's promise to Abraham. When Christ was born, Zechariah spoke of how God had remembered the Holy Covenant (Luke 1: 72). That Holy Covenant is the same as in Romans 11:27.

With the Jews committed by blood libel to the City by the Jerusalem Covenant, we can see the tremendous weight upon the present situation in the Holy Land. If you have ever been present to hear the Jewish pledge: "There will never be another holocaust, the next time we take the world with us" you can begin to understand how deeply are these commitments to Jerusalem. It is a blood covenant of life and death.

The next detail which we must observe in understanding this Covenant, it is said that the Antichrist would "confirm" it. Here the Hebrew Word "qum" is used. This word is always used when something prior is acknowledged, established, approved, or verified. Nowhere would it mean that it was drawn up or made by the Antichrist. It had already been made of record, and was simply "confirmed."

By all of these observations about this coming Covenant, certainly the present "Jerusalem Covenant" or something like it, or it's predecessor, could very well be that Covenant. I am convinced that it has the potential to be just that very thing. We will have to hide and watch to see how the future of Jerusalem works out.

THE FINAL CONSUMMATION AND COMPLETION

While the Jews are committed by a blood libel covenant to Jerusalem, the Prophet speaks of another Covenant. There would be another people other than the Jews, claiming Jerusalem at the time of the end.

They seem to be under the mesmerism of another spirit, who under the inspiration of Hell makes a blood libel *"Covenant of death."* We will find this prophecy in the 28th chapter of Isaiah, verses 14-19.

They are said to be "scornful men" who "rule" a people at that time inhabiting Jerusalem. They have made a pact of death. It is almost forced upon us to believe that the foreknowledge of God, being spoken through the Prophet Isaiah, was seeing the suicide bombers and homicide killers of today. These people have pledged themselves in a covenant of death to resist the Jews and the promise of God toward Jerusalem. Verses 15-22 must be considered to be the last seven years of Daniel's prophecy. By comparing the language used in Daniel 9:27 ("overspreading of abomination...desolate even unto the consummation, and that determined shall be poured upon the desolate") to verse 22, (a consummation, i.e. completion determined), we see the comparison. God promises to complete his Covenant work. Verses 16 and 17 show His complete work of the Covenant in that which concerns Jerusalem, or Zion.

These verses match perfectly in content and context with Isaiah 10:12: "Wherefore it shall come to pass, that when the Lord hath performed his whole work upon Mount Zion, and on Jerusalem, I will punish the front of the stout heart of the king of Assyria and the glory of his high looks." In both of these chapters we are dealing with

Babylon of the last days, and Lucifer, or Satan who inspires them.

In Isaiah 10 verses 15-22 in the final consummation, or completion, when God completes His Covenant work, these people become so rancored and scornful, hiding in a refuge of lies and falsehoods, that they make a suicide pact. It cannot be missed as we said. This has to refer to such as the "Al Aska suicide Belgrade" etc. According to these prophecies, it will take an *"overflowing scourge"* to sweep away these lies and expose the hiding places of falsehood, break the power of this *"covenant of death"* or suicide pact and put down the uprising. It is exposed that this pact is of Hell and reaches all the way to Babylon or Iraq. The Intifada against Jerusalem and the Jews is probably not going to end until a very serious crisis, called the overflowing scourge, wreaks such serious consequences as to come to a world-shaking proportion. This will put down Muslim resistance and convince the world leaders that the Jewish commitment to Jerusalem cannot be ignored. Somewhere in all of the devastation, this will bring awareness of God's Covenant, for over and over again, (85 times in the Book of Ezekiel alone) it is said "that they may know that I (not Allah) am the Lord."

It is again our learned speculation that for a brief time, that the Iraq problem, after bringing great devastation, will be settled with a short-term peace. Jerusalem will be Internationalized, allowing for the Jews to build their Temple on the North end of the Mount, the Muslims retain control of the dome, and possibly the South end be returned to its Crusader use (Revelation 11:2), for a European king to sit and administrate the international interests in Jerusalem (2 Thessalonians 2:4). A pact will be made to this effect, but will of necessity "confirm" an earlier Covenant made by the Jews over Jerusalem and in keeping with God's promise to Abraham. We believe these scenarios are immediately upon us in the present crisis in the Middle East.

We so often repeat Joseph de Coursey Jr.'s words to Hal Lindsey on TBN. Mr. de Coursey Jr. is Editor-in-Chief of the "Intelligence Digest:

> "I am convinced that what is happening in the Middle East is bringing the world to its last battle. I know nothing about the Bible. I draw my conclusions from the data we gather for the Digest."

Jesus said:

"look up and lift up thy head, for your redemption draws nigh."

THE EAST GATE AWAITS THE LORD

To close this chapter on Jerusalem and the Covenant, I am intrigued by another feature of the city, which so perfectly plays into prophecy and which has such ominous probabilities for the future of Jerusalem, and the church's eventual return to the city.

One of the most awesome sights in Jerusalem is the great Eastern Gate overlooking the Kedron Valley and the Garden of Gathsemane. There is a very interesting story and some fascinating prophecy connected with it that may serve to close this chapter on the Jerusalem Covenant and the hope of the coming Messiah.

This great gate, known in antiquity as the Golden Gate, is built squarely over the very sight of the ancient gate of Jesus' day. That gate would be the very one through which Jesus entered in the Triumphal Entry story of Matthew 21, Mark 11, and Luke 19. Both the old gate, (covered with the rubble piled high when Titus destroyed the city) and the present gate, stands ominously closed today- it's great entries filled with mortared brick and stone. It's chambers are the burial place of high-ranking Muslims, buried there in defiance to the Christian's hope of Christ's return. Taking note of the Law that prohibits any priest from crossing a graveyard, the Muslim plan was to stem any hope that the future king would enter this gate. The great walls and gates of Jerusalem, as we know them today, were built in the 7th century, and significantly refurbished by Suleiman in the 16th century. It seems the Great Gate stands with its eyes closed, oblivious to all the turmoil around it, quietly waiting for its time.

The story is told of how Suleiman the Magnificent sought to enter this gate in his day. Thinking himself to be so great as to be worthy of the title "Messiah," he prepared with great pomp to enter this very gate as the conquering King of prophecy. The night before his planned ceremony, the Lord appeared to him in a dream and warned him not to do so. The dream so unnerved him that he dropped his plans and had the East Gate sealed, as it remains today. It was a custom in the Middle East, in all the days of the great kings of the Empires, that any gate used by a King be immediately sealed and used by no other. It's use was reserved for the return of the King, which it honored. Suleimen declared the gate worthy of entrance only by the great king who last of all kings had gone through it on the Triumphal Entry. The great Golden Gate has been sealed to this day. It is the only gate in Jerusalem which is not open. According to prophecy all of the gates were to be opened to receive the great number of visitors who would tour Israel in the last days (Isaiah 60:11). However, one gate was to be closed until Jesus comes, according to Ezekiel 44.

With that background, let's turn to Ezekiel 44:2-4. Here the Prophet, while viewing the future Jerusalem and measuring it for record, comes to the East Gate of our day. Notice his specific words. "It was shut." This puzzled him until the Lord explained:

> *This gate shall be shut, it shall not be opened, and no man shall enter in by it; because the Lord, the God of Israel, hath entered in by it, therefore it shall be shut.*

You see how perfect God's foreknowledge is and how well He watches over His word to fulfill it. And when will the gate again be opened?

It is for the prince; the prince, he shall sit in it ...

That great gate sits on the Eastern side of the Mount, as it were with its eyes closed, indifferent and oblivious to all the commotion around, calmly waiting for the real Peacemaker to come. In all due respect to the good efforts of well-intentioned men, there will be no peace in the Middle East, or anywhere else, until a world wakes up to receive the real Maker of Peace, the Prince of Peace, the Lord of Lords, the King of Kings. Jesus the Christ is His name.

No wonder the Psalms sing of that day with such triumph:

Lift up your heads, o ye gates; and be ye lifted up, ye everlasting doors; and the King of glory shall come in. Who is the King of glory? The Lord strong and mighty, the Lord mighty in battle.

Lift up your heads, o ye gates; even lift them up, ye everlasting doors; and the King of glory shall come in. Who is the King of glory? The Lord of Hosts, he is the King of glory. Selah.

All through the city of Jerusalem, you will see this hope championed. Signs will greet you on every turn: "WELCOME MESSIAH."

The city, and yes a world of believers, are preparing for His soon return.

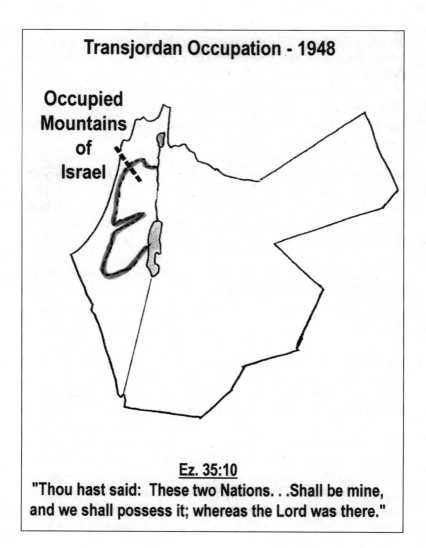

Transjordan Occupation - 1948

Occupied Mountains of Israel

Ez. 35:10
"Thou hast said: These two Nations. . .Shall be mine, and we shall possess it; whereas the Lord was there."

THE JERUSALEM COVENANT

Signed by the Heads of State of Israel and affirmed by Jews world-wide.

AS OF THIS DAY...Jerusalem Day, the twenty-eighth day of the month of Iyar in the year five thousand seven hundred fifty-two; One thousand nine hundred and twenty-two years after the destruction of the Second Temple; forty-five years since the founding of the state of Israel; twenty-five years since the Six Day War during which the Israel Defense Forces, in defense of our very existence, restored the Temple Mount and the unity of Jerusalem; twelve years since the Knesset of Israel reestablished Jerusalem, "unified and whole, as the Capital of Israel," "the State of Israel is the State of the Jewish People" and the Capital of the People of Israel.

We have gather together in Zion, sovereign national officials and leaders of our communities everywhere to enter into a covenant with Jerusalem, as was done by the leaders of our nation and all the people of Israel upon Israel's return to our Land from Babylonian exile wherein the people and their leaders vowed to "dwell in Jerusalem, the Holy City."

ONCE AGAIN..."Our feet stand within your gates, O Jerusalem-- Jerusalem built as a city joined together" which "unites the people of Israel to one another," and "links heavenly Jerusalem with earthly Jerusalem."

WE HAVE RETURNED...to the place that the Lord vowed to bestow upon the descendants of Abraham, Father of our Nation; to the City of David, King of Israel; where Solomon, son of David, built a Holy Temple and a Capital City; which with time became the Mother of all Israel; a City and the Mother of all enactments of Justice and Righteousness, and for the wisdom and insights of the ancient world; where a Second Temple was erected in the days of Ezra and Nehemiah.

In this city the prophets of the Lord prophesied; in this City our Sages taught Torah; in the City of Sanhedrin convened in session in its stone chamber. "For here were the seat of justice and the Throne of the House of David," "for out of Zion shall go forth Toray, and the Word of the Lord from Jerusalem."

TODAY AS OF OLD...we hold fast to the truth of the words of the Prophets of Israel, that all the inhabitants of this world shall enter within the gates of Jerusalem: "All it shall come to pass in the end of days, the mountain of the House of the Lord will be well established at the peak of the mountains and will tower above the hills, and all the nations shall stream towards it."

Each and every nation will live by its own faith: "For all the people will go forward,k each with its own Divine Name: we shall go in the name of the Lord our God ever and ever." And in this Spirit, the Knesset of the State of Israel has enacted a law establishing: the places holy to the peoples of all religions shall be protected from any desecration and from any restriction of free access to them.

JERUSALEM...Peace and tranquility shall reign in the city: "Pray for the peace of Jerusalem; may those that love you be tran-quil. May there be peace within your walls, and tranquility within your palaces." Out of Jerusalem a message of peace went forth and shall yet go forth again to all the inhabitants of the earth: "And they shall beat their swords into plowshares, and their spears into pruning-hooks; Nations will not lift up sword against nation or shall they learn war any more." Our sages, of blessed memory, have said: In the future The Holy One, the Blessed can comfort Jerusalem only with peace."

FROM THIS PLACE...we once again take our vow: "If I forget thee, O Jerusalem, may my right hand lose its strength; may my tongue stick to my palate if I do not remember you, If I do not raise up Jerusalem at the very height of my rejoicing."

AND WITH ALL THIS UNDERSTANDINGS...we enter into this covenant and write: We shall bind you to us forever, we shall bind you to us with faithfulness, with righteousness and justice, with steadfast love and compassion. We love you O Jerusalem with eternal love, with unbound love, under siege and when liberated from the yoke of oppressors: we have been martyred for you, we have clung to you. Our faithfulness to you we shall bequeath to our children after us. Forever more, our home shall be within you.

IN CERTIFICATION OF THIS COVENANT, WE SIGN

CHAPTER 5

PARTING OF THE LAND

"..and parted my land" (Joel 3:20)
"..appointed my land into their possession"
(Ezekiel 36:5)

On October 22, 2001, a young Palestinian woman said over Palestinian T.V.:

"All we ask is that (Arab) countries stand by our side, give us weapons, and we, on our own, will...kill them...murder them...slaughter them, all of them. We won't spare a single Jew."

Over the same TV station and at the same time, there came a call for more terror from Moslem Minister Zayed bin Sultan Aal Nahyan. His sermon at the Mosque in Gaza included these words:

The Jews are Jews, whether Labor or Likud...they are all liars..Oh brother believers, the criminals, the terrorists are the Jews. They are the ones who must be butchered and killed, as Allah the Almighty said, fight them. Allah will torture them at your hands, and will humiliate them and will help you to overcome them, and will relieve the

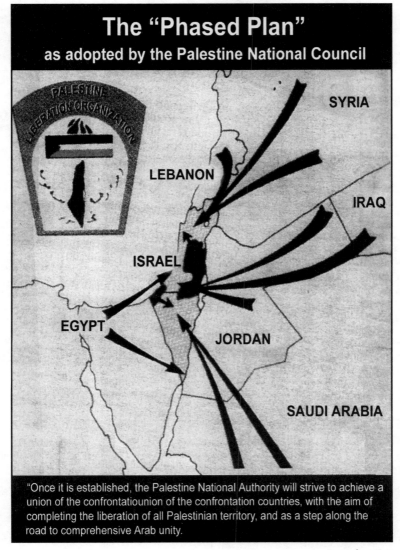

The "Phased Plan"
as adopted by the Palestine National Council

"Once it is established, the Palestine National Authority will strive to achieve a union of the confrontatiounion of the confrontation countries, with the aim of completing the liberation of all Palestinian territory, and as a step along the road to comprehensive Arab unity.

minds of the believers. We fight in the path of Allah and kill and are killed. The Jews are the allies of the Christians – no matter where they are found. Fight them, wherever you are. Wherever you meet them, kill them. Kill those Jews and those Americans who are like them.

These examples of perpetuated hate are only two of thousands of references that are driving the Muslim world against the Jews and all who support them. This kind of hate cannot be rationalized nor reasoned with, and certainly cannot be tolerated in any civil society.

The question must be addressed: - how can such hate be justified and how can religious leaders promote it? Where did it start, and where will it end? At the closing of this article, we will answer these questions and show that this is a 4000-year-old hate, clearly prophesied in the Bible to be the menace-causing terror in the last days.

Partitioning of the land has received wide coverage in our news today. Every day the world is on the brink of disaster, and this crisis is all over the land of Israel and the "partitioning" of that land.

BACKGROUND OF THE PARTITION

Much of the material found in this chapter will seem to be redundant from the second chapter. However, in chapter two, the subject was about Jordan's involvement in the

West Bank problem. In this chapter it will be necessary to refer to some of the same information, but hope to approach the subject from the standpoint of the parting of the land itself and its prophetic implications.

At the end of WWII, after the Arabs and the Ottoman Empire, which controlled all the Mid-East for 500 years prior to 1919, joined Hitler's cause, Allied troops were given mandate over various parts of the Area. Britain, who had earlier acted in favor of a Jewish State in the Holy Land, and persuaded the League of Nations to mandate the same, was given mandate over Palestine. The area known as Palestine then included what are now the States of Jordan, Lebanon, and Israel. There was no Palestinian State, nor was there a West Bank in the partition of that land. The "Palestinian State" was considered Trans-Jordan, (across the Jordan). West of the Jordan River, although the border was left a little vague, was generally accepted as mandated to be a Jewish State. When Israel, by UN mandate was allowed to become a Nation in November of 1947, and declared herself an Independent Nation in May of 1948, seven Arab nations attacked, intending to drive her to the sea and destroy the new nation. When the War of Independence was over, Israel had secured all her borders except those with the state of Trans-Jordan. Trans-Jordan had pressed into the mountainous part of Israel and taken it all, including the city of Jerusalem. Jews were immediately killed or driven out of these areas, Synagogues and other holy Jewish and

Christian sites were destroyed, Jerusalem and the Temple Mount was occupied and the Jewish section of Jerusalem on Zion was cut off.

Trans-Jordan changed its name and became simply "Jordan," dropping the "Trans," because it intended to possess land on both sides of the Jordan River. Its intentions were to annex the "Territories" on the West Side of Jordan, calling it the West Bank of Jordan. The East Side of the Jordan River would become simply Jordan. They intended two separate countries all under the King of Jordan.

Such unrest was created over the Annex of the West Bank, that Jordan decided to drop plans for an annex, and in the vacuum, left the West Bank in the hands of the Revolutionaries. Over the years, Arabs from 29 different Arab countries had moved into the area to take advantage of jobs and an affluent society which had been created by the industry of the Jewish State. Before this, a Palestinian was anyone living in Palestine – namely Jews, Arabs, Christians, etc.

Therefore, many, if not most of the leadership of the Palestinians are not native to the land of Israel at all. Even Mr. Yasser Arafat is not a "Palestinian." He is an Egyptian born Revolutionary, trained in the former Soviet Union, and sent from the Soviets with their blessing to take advantage of the vacuum in the territories and to destabilize the Jewish State.

At the invitation of his cousin, Mufti-Hag Amin al

Husseine, who was at the time Mofti of Jerusalem, Yasser Arafat came into the picture. He quickly became spokesman for the West Bank. Capitalizing upon an already volatile situation, and using the power of an old religious animosity between the Jews and the Arabs, he aggravated the smoldering "Palestinian" rebellion against Israel already boiling under the surface. With a great amount of anti-Israel sentiment in the international institutions, namely Europe and the UN, he simply used the discontent of the immigrant Arabs in the territories to organize the "PLO" (Palestinian Liberation Organization). In doing so he has played upon an ancient hate, sewn into the Arab populous ever since Ishmael, and has precipitated an acute hate and disdain for the Jewish State. That hate is now out of control. Out of this revolution and engendered hate, has come several very volatile terrorist groups more rebellious than their progenitors.

In June of 1976, when two Arab states, namely Syria and Egypt, attacked Israel again intending to destroy the state, Jordan was persuaded to join them. Israel soundly defeated them in what has been called the "Six Day War." The Golan Heights was taken from Syria, the Sinai taken from Egypt, and the West Bank with Jerusalem, was taken back from Jordanian occupation.

Israel now possesses all of the Promised Land of Prophecy, but the "Raging Nations" of the anti-Christ, anti-God, anti-Israel world are determined to unseat

Israel from her Holy sites. Because of the foothold gained into the State of Israel by the revolutionary factions of world revolution, Israel has been under constant demand to defend her borders.

The Western media (in the United States), Britain and Europe conveniently and consistently overlook the true background of the partition problem. Never do they admit to the fact that the West Bank, (or Territories), were actually part of the original Partition and Mandate which included every country of the Mid-East as we know them today. The UN, under control of Soviet-leaning bias, and catering heavily toward Arab and Muslim cause, (blackmailed by oil interests) refuses to face its own responsibility for the confusion by not clarifying the borders of the Mandate. The Western media, in a propagation of a sheer lie, continues to say that Israel is "occupying" the West Bank. Western political leaders and the UN have conveniently adopted this possession. It is that adoption that is at the heart of the whole problem today.

After WW II, the Allies were given Mandate over the Middle East. As we have said, England was given Mandate over Palestine. "Palestine" then included all of what we now know as Jordan and Israel. When the Balfour Proclamation came forth, such an uprising ensued, that Britain quickly divided the "Palestinian State" into two parts. East of the Jordan River was called "Transjordan" and was given to the Palestinians and West of the Jordan River was mandated to the Jews for a "homeland for the Jews."

The League of Nations confirmed this arrangement, and later in 1947, the UN also made mandate of the same. Israel's internationally accepted border was the Jordan River. However, the State of Transjordan immediately attacked Israel, pressed into the mountainous part of the State of Israel and took possession of it, including the old city of Jerusalem and the Temple Mount. Israel, just a new nation and fighting five Muslim nations on every side, was unable to stop the Jordanian Army. Transjordan annexed the Territories and changed her name to "Jordan" and called herself the "West Bank of Jordan" and "Jordan proper."

Jordan occupied the West Bank and Jerusalem until 1967. In the Six-Day War, Israel retook the West Bank and Jerusalem, and ended the Jordanian Occupation. However, the Western media, in a propagation of a sheer lie, continues to say that Israel is "occupying" the West Bank.

Western political leaders and the UN have conveniently adopted this possession. It is that adoption that is at the heart of the whole problem today.

Let's look at this whole scenario from Biblical Prophetic perspective.

WEST BANK IN BIBLE PERSPECTIVE

It is clearly established in the prophecy of hundreds of

scriptures that God would set a second time to gather his people Israel from the Four Corners of the world. It is also clearly prophesied by scores of Scriptures that they would be returned to their "borders." It is those borders that are in such conflict today and creating a world crisis of terrorism.

There is some debate as to the exact borders of the return. Abraham was promised certain lands, which he could view from Bethel. These were promised to Isaac and his seed and were known as the Covenant Promised Land. In addition to Isaac's promise, all of Abraham's seed was promised larger borders, which takes in the entire Middle East. These lands were given to Ishmael and the sons of Keturah, Abraham's wife after the death of Sarai. Joshua never possessed some of the Promised Land.

David's Kingdom set a new concept of borders. There were the borders that became established in the return from Babylon. Then there are the borders of the present return. These must differ from the Kingdom Promise concerning Israel in the Millennium. A full return of the Jews to the Land will take place when the present diplomacy of peace agreements breaks down completely, and the Armies of the Nations will surround Israel. I am only going to concern us with the borders now in question, namely the borders of this present return. Following are texts that can be clearly identified with the present return of the Jews and the establishment of the State of Israel as we know it today.

God, through the Prophet Jeremiah, promised that Israel would *"come again to their own border."* (Jeremiah 31:17) Those borders are also described in Ezekiel 37:25. This whole chapter is unquestionably concerned with the re-establishment of the state of Israel in our day. These borders, according to Ezekiel 37:25 are directly comparable to the borders mandated both by the Balfour Proclamation, the League of Nations mandate in 1922, and the UN mandate in 1967. They are the expected borders of Israel today.

JORDAN DIVIDES THE LAND

In Joel 1:6, God complains that "a nation has come upon my land." This event is dated by verse 15 and is shown to be in the "day of the Lord" which is "at hand." Herein lies the root of all of the conflict today, and the makings of the very scenario prophesied for the last days.

In several texts which are concerned with the borders of Israel in the return, the prophetic finger is pointed at Jordan for the cause of Israel's grief and the international pressure upon her to part the land. For instance, Amos 1:13 names Gaza and Lebanon as part with Jordan in the transgressions against the "borders" of Israel. Then it points directly to Jordan (Ammon): "For the transgression of Ammon, I will not turn away the punishment thereof: (Why?) because they have enlarged their border."

As we have shown, it was Jordan who took the West Bank from the State of Israel in 1947 and then sought to annex it, therefore "enlarging" their "borders." Ezekiel 11:15 speaks of a people (inhabitants of Jerusalem), who would say:

"While you were away from the Lord, (in the Diaspora,) *this land was given us to possess."*

These "inhabitants" relate to today's Palestinians in the Muslim section of old Jerusalem and in all of the East part of Jerusalem. In the next two verses God admits that he did scatter them but that He would be to them a "little sanctuary" (a limited blessing), and that He would gather them again, and, "Give you the land of Israel"

So we see that these "Palestinians" (having come to Israel from 29 different countries) are the people of the nations who have come upon His land, and are the "inhabitants of Jerusalem" who are saying "while you were driven out of the land, the land has become our inheritance."

If Muslims would but read their own book they would see that they are contrary, not only to God's will, but contrary to the teachings of their own acclaimed "prophet" Mohammed. In the Koran, - Sura five, "the tables," it clearly states Mohammed's expectation. It teaches:

1.   The Holy Land is West of the Jordan.

2. Foresees the return of the Jews to this land in the last days.

3. Says the land is reserved for the Jews.

4. Blesses the Jews in the Land.

5. Says all of this would be in the last days.

Therefore, we see that the "parting of the land" is contrary even to the Muslim's Holy Book.

Ezekiel Chapters 34 through 36 are entirely given to the subject of the "Mountains of Israel." When we do a little homework and outline on a topo map the mountainous areas of the Holy Land, or the State of Israel, one will discover that these "Mountains of Israel" are exactly comparable to the West Bank.

PERPETUAL HATE

As we study the text carefully, we discover that just as in many other texts, Amman, (Edom, Moab and Ammon, or Mt. Seir, which is in Jordan), are the aggressors, who out of Perpetual Hate, (i.e. hate that is taught and perpetuated) cause bloody terrorism against Israel (Ezekiel 35:5).

It is important to remember that Mt. Seir in Jordan, (down near Petra), was the home of Esau, the brother of Jacob. Esau and his family lived in the barren wasteland while Jacob and his sons lived in the "land of milk and honey." A perpetual hate for Jacob, heir of promise, was passed on from generation to generation as the jealousy of Esau turned to acute resentment. We can be sure that each generation of Edomites heard the story told in anger and bitterness how that Jacob stole the birthright and the blessing from his brother Esau. It was plainly said that Isaac had been tricked, and that the land of blessing (i.e. the Holy Land) should, by right of birthright, belong to Esau and his descendants.

Hate, resentment and bitterness always creates a profane person, (Hebrews 12: 15-17) and these attitudes are transferred to many generations of a family. God himself marked Esau as a very "profane" person. Esau's resistance of the Israelites possession of the Holy Land began as far back as Moses, when he sought to lead Israel into the Promised Land. Their first resistance was Edom, who refused to let them cross. The history of Edom shows them to be a very treacherous, quarrelsome people always ready to throw the Jews out of the land. It was Edom who joined Moab and Ammon (the same as Jordan today), to destroy Israel and Jerusalem in Jehoshaphat's day. And it will be in that same place of their destruction that again God will deal with them (Joel 3:1-2). When Babylon burned Jerusalem it was Edom who stood close by and cried *"raze it, raze it, even to the foundation thereof"* (Psalm137:7).

In the return from Babylon, the Jews had to continually fight the Edomites while rebuilding the second Temple. The Herods were "Idumeans," the Roman name for the Edomites. When Titus destroyed Jerusalem in AD 70,

Josephus recorded that the Idumeans were "naturally a most barbarous and bloody nation" ("Wars" book 4, ch. 5). Evidently they are doomed to forever carry that hate, resentment and bitterness. Ezekiel finds them the same in these days of return - for, in dealing with the inhabitants of the "Mountains of Israel" (or in our terms, the West Bank), he records the Lord saying:

> *"Son of man, set thy face against Mount Seir* (Edom or Jordan today), *because thou hast had perpetual hatred and shed the blood of the children of Israel by the force of the sword in the time of their calamity..."* (emphasis mine)

Let's clear up confusion being propagated by the Western Press. The hate, which is so evident among the people in the West Bank, is not because of poverty (this is a worn-out old cliche of Liberal bias), nor is it because of oppression, nor is it out of desperation. It cannot be viewed as simply political descent against an occupying and oppressive State. It is however a deeply ingrained hate taught and propagated since Esau hated Jacob for stealing the birthright and the blessing. Trained Revolutionary factions today perpetuate hate even in schools and textbooks, whipping up the youth to a frenzy level. Add to this the religious fervor of Clerics of Islam who make the destruction of Israel Allah's priority, and promise great bliss in the afterworld if one becomes a martyr. Then add the involvement from rogue regimes, which promise a fortune to the family which sacrifices a child to homoside death so that those parents take pride in the child's suicide death, and encourages the child to die for the family's sake, and you now have a "perpetuated hate" or "perpetual hate."

Ezekiel 35 verse 10 points directly to the present situation in Israel and is so accurate that it is startling. At what other time in Jordan's history has the country claimed two countries as it's own? Only when "Transjordan" possessed the Mountains of Israel in Israel's War of Independence, then decided to annex it and make itself two countries in one, namely the West Bank of Jordan and Jordan proper on the East side of Jordan. However they have overlooked one little detail, not taking into consideration that the God of Israel was involved and would not tolerate the dividing of the land. So we read: "..whereas the Lord was there" (verse 10).

In the 36th chapter of Ezekiel, God personifies the Mountains of Israel, or the West Bank, and ancient high places. God speaks to them about the "enemy" (v. 2) that said; "Aha, even the ancient high places are ours in possession." The Hebrew word for "possession" here is moreshah, which means "to receive by inheritance." Herein is the very crux of the issue in Israel today. Jordan, and through it the entire Arab world, is claiming the ancient high place, the Temple Mount, as theirs by inheritance. The WAFK of Jordan, overseers of the Temple Mount today, will not let a single Jew on the Mount. This was highlighted in September of 2001, when Ariel Sharon simply visited the Temple Mount. Out of rebellion to that single visit by a Jew (the first and only official visit in 2000 years) Arafat organized the Al Asqu Martyr Brigade, which has been responsible for scores of suicide or homicide bombings to date.

In verse 3 of the same chapter, God accuses the Palestinians that they "swallowed you," or in the NIV, "ravaged you and hounded you from every side so that you became the possession of the rest of the nations and the object of people's malicious talk and slander." That is precisely the headline news day after day in our current situation. The *"residue of the heathen"* (KJV), or *"rest of the nations"* (NIV), describes perfectly the Palestinians today, very few of which are actual residents of the West Bank area, but are from 29 different nations who have the backing of the *"rest of the nations."*

Again in verse 5, God accuses "Idumea" or Jordan, because they had "appointed my land into their possession." The Amplified Version reads thus, *"given to themselves my land with wholehearted joy and with utmost contempt."* A perfect depiction of Arafat and his terrorist cohorts can be found in the King James Version: *"despiteful minds."*

THE WEST BANK AND ISRAEL
SAME IN THE BIBLE

In verse 6 it is made clear that the Mountains of Israel and the State of Israel in God's mind are the same. In verse 7, God declares that in the end the *"heathen that are about you, they shall bear their shame."* From verse 8 God recalls the Diaspora and prophesies the future for the West Bank of Judea and Samaria, God will *"settle you after your old estates."* (v.11) *"cities will be inhabited, and the wasted shall be built."* (v.10) The West Bank problem will not end until God intervenes and establishes Israel to her ancient rights to the land.

Verse 12 declares the day to come when *"even my people Israel"* shall *"possess thee, and thou shalt be their inheritance."* The *"old estates"* established in Joshua's day have been evident since then, being clearly marked by rock walls. Those rock walls can be seen today throughout the West Bank. They are the *"old estates"* of Judea and Samaria.

I think we have commented enough on these chapters to sufficiently show what God's Word has to say about the Mountains of Israel and the West Bank.

PARTED MY LAND

Joel chapter 3 confronts the very problem of the West Bank today and brings us dramatically up to events that are soon to take place in Israel. Here the specific time for the following events are set:

"..in those days and in that time when I shall bring again the captivity of Judah and Jerusalem...."

This terminology is used specifically for the return of Israel to the land in the last days. That points the text to our very time.

From the present conflict, eventually all nations must become involved in certain negotiations, which will be designed to "plead with" the world's armies. And what is the "pleading" to accomplish? "For my people, and for my heritage Israel." And what is the issue prophesied which will bring all nations to negotiations in the Middle East? We are specifically told it is because they have, "PARTED MY LAND." This is a direct reference to the "Partition of the Land," or "Land for Peace" policies in today's negotiations being forced upon Israel by the UN, the EU, and even the United States.

In Zephaniah 1:14, we find reference to the West Bank. This is mentioned in relationship to the day of the coming of the Lord. We see that the rest is referring to the same as Joel 3. The text also shows that it is in reference to the Return of the Jews (2:1, 2). It is also in reference to the day of the fierce anger of the Lord (verses 15 and 18). These references also point directly again to Moab, and Ammon, (Jordan today), and the border problem (chapter 2 verse 8). All of this places it in perfect alignment with today's events.

We find mention of the Palestinians in verse 5, the rogue name given to the Holy Land by the Emperor Hadrian in order to wipe out all memory of Biblical Israel.

Gaza and Ashkelon are also mentioned. Both of these cities are primary in the Palestinian cause today. In this reference let's look at the following:

> *I have heard the reproach of Moab, and the revilings of the children of Ammon, whereby they have reproached my people, and magnified themselves against their borders* (Zephaniah 2:8).

Again, both Moab and Ammon are modern day Jordan. The "Cherethites" of verse 5 would also indicate the area of Jordan in-as-much as, according to Smith's Bible Dictionary, Chereth is a brook near Beth-Shean, just across the Jordan River from Jericho and in the territory of Jordan. We do not need to elaborate again, that Jordan created the West Bank problem, and is very much involved in the "revilings and reproach of the Palestinians" against Israel today. And true to this prophecy, they certainly have "magnified themselves against" the borders of Israel.

ANTICHRIST DIVIDES THE LAND FOR GAIN

Another clear reference to the Parting of the Land of Israel in the last days can be found in Daniel's prophecy. Chapter 11:36-39 expounds upon the Antichrist when he comes to power. His relationship to the Land of Israel is clear. He is a hater of the Jews and despises the Abrahamic covenant (v.30). He takes away the daily sacrifices, which will be re-established on the Temple Mount for a short time during the first part of the Tribulation. He shall *"enter the glorious* (Holy) *Land"* (v.41).

Verse 39 records that he will "divide the land for gain" since his interest is the Holy Land, where he will establish his throne (Thessalonians 2:4). This probably will be part of the Covenant that the Antichrist will confirm (Daniel 9:27). A Covenant between the UN and Israel, and agreed to by the world's nations, will divide the land, internationalize Jerusalem- cutting it in half (Zechariah chapters12 and 14), and allow both Jew and Arab rights to the Temple Mount (Revelation 11:2). I am persuaded this speaks of the pre-ponderant problem as it is today. Eventually, the portion of the land will still be an issue in Antichrist's day.

The final result of this present crisis is seen in Zechariah 14: 9-17. A covenant of peace will follow mass destruction in the Middle East. The land will be partitioned into a Palestinian State with Jerusalem being divided, (Zechariah 14:2), and for a short 3 1/2 years it will seem some relief has come to the war-torn Middle East. However, the internationalizing of Jerusalem and the compromising of the Temple Mount will only lead to a European King's boldness to set himself up as God (2 Thessalonians 2:7). A new onslaught against Israel will bring the Lord's direct intervention (Zechariah 14:4); the Battle of Armageddon will ensue and the Beast and his Antichrist will be destroyed (Zechariah 14, and Revelation chapters 16, and 19).

A 4000-YEAR-OLD HATE

Earlier we referred to questions that have so plagued the Palestinian/Israeli issue today. Why is there such rancor, malice, and bitterness in the hearts of the Palestinian people? Why can the world's finest diplomats find no rational solution? This hate persists even though it threatens total holocaust to the entire world.

Western Media and those sympathetic to the Palestinian cause promote every excuse. One of the prime excuses for suicide homicide is the hopelessness of the financial and social despair that these people are in because of Israeli oppression. In fact, it is not the Israeli people that put them in such shape, but their own leaders. These people came from 29 different Muslim countries, each one every bit as oppressive as the Palestinian area. That is why they came to Israel. It was to take advantage of the job market that Israeli industry was providing. They were put to work by the thousands, until terrorism forced the closure of the borders of the West Bank, making it impossible to enter Israel and get to their job sites. If terror would cease, the job market would open up to them again. What is it then that causes millions to come to Israel and America seeking prosperity, and then inspires them to destroy the very people who feed them? I am prepared to give that answer.

In referring to Hebrews 12:14-16, we find this answer. In this text we are told to work for peace with all people.

Our blessed America is seeking, at it's own peril, to obey this commandment. We support all peace efforts by our government in the war against terrorism. Howbeit we are not encouraged by the prospects of peace?

Then Paul exhorts us to *"look diligently"* (e.g. see to it, give careful and painstaking care) lest *"bitterness"* springing up, defile many. For an example of this kind of rancor and bitterness, Paul refers to Esau, that *"profane person"* who traded his birthright for a *"morsel of meat,"* and then hated his brother and family for it. Even though Isaac and the Lord would have shown no favoritism, and Isaac blessed both Esau and Jacob (Hebrews 11:20); and even though Esau did receive the portion of the firstborn of the inheritance of Isaac, still he allowed unforgiveness to fill his soul with malevolence and hostility and finally malice, against Jacob and the Covenant promise.

Esau's hate became so deep that he was not able to stop its malicious, bitter rancor against his brother. He knew it was wrong just as those today know it is wrong. He allowed his soul to get warped with that hate, that even when he tried to repent, and cried out to God with tears, he could not find any real repentance because he could not or would not forgive. We fear his tears were not sincere, but tears of self-pity.

In his deep hate he promoted to his family ill feelings against the Jews. That hate has been propagated in the hearts of the Edomites ever since. They have joined a like-hate also propagated among the family of another of Abraham's sons, Ishmael (father of the Arabs) who himself found equal and similar reasons to hate the family of Isaac. From this, a whole society of people have been impregnated with a deep and perpetuated hate for the Jew. As Paul warned, the root of bitterness springing up, has and is, defiling many today. This can be seen easily when we realize that Esau is Edom and Mt. Seir of the Bible, and therefore are the Jordanian people of today. Also remember that it was Jordan that created the West Bank problem and it is the Jordanian Palestinians who are showing such hate and rancor against the sons of Jacob today.

No wonder when God, through the prophet Ezekiel, reveals to us this West Bank problem which would plague Israel in the latter day return, that he would finger "Mt. Seir" which is modern day Jordan (Ezekiel 35:2). It is the same *"old hate"* which Ezekiel also spoke about in the 25th chapter, verse 15. Here, in union with the Ammonites (v.1) and *"Edom"* (v.14) and joined by the *"Philistines"* (present day Gaza) they exercise spite against the land of Israel (v.6) and defile the sanctuary (v.3) and take *"vengeance with a spiteful heart."* All of this is because of an "OLD HATRED," the old hatred of Esau and Ishmael.

As far as can be ascertained, the Philistines disappeared as a people by that name. At least they were never mentioned again as a threat to Israel after the Assyrian invasion. The prophecy in Ezekiel 25 is surely a latter day prophecy, as Ezekiel prophesied no later than the captivity that was brought on by Nebuchadnezzer during the return from Babylon. It is interesting that the Philistine would be mentioned since it is their namesake's people that are defying God's plan in the land of Israel today.

EXHORTATION FOR US TODAY

As a spiritual lesson to us, consider this ancient hate that has caused constant turmoil in the Middle East for 4000 years. Consider too how much may be going on in our own lives and in some of our churches simply because of some "OLD HATE." Maybe something in our past has been unfair, and we have been seriously wronged. Maybe something that someone said or did caused animosity to rise in our soul. Instead of forgiving and forgetting, we let it get to us. We began to be bitter and to retaliate, allowing malice to enter our hearts. Malice is an act with intent to hurt and anger, and soon hate, took over our total emotions. Now we cannot bring ourselves to forgive or repent, because we do not or will not give up our justified anger, even though we have prayed and sought deliverance with tears. Our bitterness may be causing all kinds of psychological or emotional problems. To cope with it we may turn to drugs, but as soon as the drug wears off, the old hate takes over. We are tearing up our church, family, marriage, and friendships to accommodate our anger. We may have gone so far as to have allowed our hate and anger to go too deep, and like Esau, we may have become incurable.

Philo, the great Philosopher of Alexandria said "The diseases of the soul are almost totally incurable, if not completely incurable." Esau found it so and so may you or I if we continue to let those diseases of the soul; rancor, jealousy, malice, anger, hate, bitterness, etc. dominate our soul. SELAH!

Back to the Palestinian problem with the descendants of Esau. Never has the prophecy of the Bible been more relative and meaningful. Are you ready and looking for the coming of the Lord, the great God of our salvation?

"Behold he cometh with clouds, and every eye shall see Him, and they also which pierced Him: and all kindred's of the earth shall wail because of Him. Even so, Amen."

The final prayer of the Bible is *"even so come Lord Jesus"* (Revelation 22:20).

CHAPTER 6

JUDGMENT
IN THE MIDDLE EAST

HOW GOD WINDS IT UP

Historian Will Durant once said: "Of the 3400 years of recorded history of the human race, there have been approximately 269 years of peace." Although there is much talk of peace in our time, we have seen very little of it. The Prophet Jeremiah observed: *"Peace, peace when there is no peace"* (Jeremiah 6:14, 8:ll). Isaiah said: *"there is no peace to the wicked saith my God"* (Isaiah 48:22, 57:21).

The Apostle Paul warned us of the last days: *"For when they shall say 'peace and safety', then sudden destruction cometh upon them, as travail upon a woman with child, and they shall not escape"* (1 Thessalonians 5:3). So it seems we are in that very day.

I am not a date-setter. It creates such confusion in the Church, not to mention the world around us. When, for the sake of sensationalism, someone sets a date for certain prophetic events to occur, it makes mockery of the truth of the Word of God. It confuses the whole matter. I am not a prophet nor the son of a prophet. However, whenever someone gives a specific date for something to happen, I can confidently prophesy that it will not happen at that time. Jesus plainly told us we would not know the day nor the hour, and it was not for us to speculate about the exact times of prophetic events (Acts 1:7). On the other hand, Our Lord said that we ought to be able to read the signs of the times (Matthew 16:3). He said not to be able to read the "times and seasons" would make us "hypocrites." That is a very strong indictment of which we hope not to be guilty.

By making a careful study of the "signs of the times" as specifically declared in the prophecies, and by comparing these prophecies with the present world scene, I am forced to say at least 'the time is at hand.' We are in the "times and seasons." What, with the Jerusalem Covenant confirmed, and with its absolute statement of unwavering commitment on the part of World Jewry to Jerusalem as the forever capital of the Jewish people and the State of Israel; and with the peace negotiations to consider the status of Jerusalem; and knowing the firm resolve of Arafat, and the Palestinians to make Jerusalem their capitol; and with the highly explosive situation in the Middle East which threatens to involve the whole world in nuclear war, you can easily see why I am tempted to say, "if the tribulation does not start very soon, it will have missed an excellent opportunity." However, it will come in God's time.

While the world is rejoicing and politicians are gaining political mileage out of the present peace initiatives, serious flaws are being conveniently ignored. At least two serious questions remain unanswered:

1. How can Israel negotiate away any part of the Mountains of Israel, known to us as the West Bank? Both for security reasons, and by the fact that God has clearly stated in his Word that such negotiations will come to naught, such intentions will lead to chaos. As we have shown earlier, to trade off the West Bank would be to divide from God's promise some very significant Biblical spots, such as:

BETHEL- Where Jacob saw heaven and the spot where Abraham was standing when he was told that he could have everything from there Eastward, Westward, Northward and Southward.

HEBRON- Where Abraham, Isaac, and Rebecca are buried.

BETHLEHEM- Where David had his home, and where Jesus was born.

SHILO- Where the Ark rested and the Tabernacle stood until moved to Solomon's new Temple.

JERUSALEM- Where the Temple stood, where our Lord was crucified, and Capital of the State of Israel for 3000 years.

At least six times in prophecy, God said he would settle this border problem over the Mountains of Israel.

2. The Jerusalem Problem must be settled once and for all. No peace negotiations in the area are worth consideration until this is accomplished. Jewish claim to Jerusalem in the Jerusalem Covenant, the State of Israel's claims to it as their capitol, Jordan's formidable control over the Temple Mount, (which angers the PLO) and the Palestinian demand that it be designated as the Capital of the new Palestinian State, sets a very volatile scenario. Add to this the historic background of deeply set religious commitments on behalf of the Muslims, Jews and Christians, especially the great Catholic church with all of its interests in Jerusalem: commitments which each hold in the name of their God, and are well ready to die for. We can see why the situation is far from settled.

GOD'S CHALLENGE TO THE UN

In the book of Isaiah Chapter 41, we find an interesting challenge, which we believe we can show belongs to the days of Israel's return and the invitation to enter into debate issued by the Lord himself. The commentators all put this text into the context of the Idol Gods of Israel's former time. But the whole chapter concerns God's call to Israel, and His care over them. The verses just prior to our text in consideration are unquestionably prophecies concerning the renewal of the land in Israel's final return.

Therefore it makes the ones spoken of not the old idols of past times but the present idols who confront Israel and her right to exist. Those idols today which present their cause are not idols of stone or wood, but of flesh and bone. They are men and women in the high councils of our world who are revered as Gods by an ungodly world. They take council against the Lord and his Christ and question their claim to Zion and the Holy Land (Psalms 2). They could well be the councils of the UN and its 200 plus nations of the General Assembly which questions the very right of Israel to exist in the land.

In that context let's note the challenge that God puts forth to the Nations of the World. "Come on" he says, "present your case." "Set forth your arguments, says the King of Jacob." "Prophesy, tell us what is going to happen." And then, because so much of Israel's future depends on an understanding of the past, God challenged them to "tell us what the past has been, so that we may know the final outcome."

Our world leaders sit today in judgment upon Israel and the Holy Land as if they were Gods, and certainly in

defiance of God and His plan for the area. They deliber-
ate and debate about the land and it's future, never considering either the Bible record of the past and God's
promise for the future, nor the recent history of the problem. So they are making bad judgments which our God
will soon challenge. In the end they will be "less than
nothing" and their words *"utterly worthless"* (v.24).

But until God intervenes, along with Israel, we must
endure their foolishness and misjudgment in the Middle
East.

WORLD ARMIES SCHEDULED TO SURROUND JERUSALEM

I would not presume to detail the events of the next few
years in the Middle East. I can say with absolute certainty
however, that in the very near future, the Multi-national
forces, called the Armies of the Nations in Scripture, will
gather around Jerusalem (Joel 3:1-2). Just as 35 nations of
troops were twice summoned to deal with the Saddam
Hussein problem, the crisis now brewing in Israel will
require the same kind of international intervention. Our
allies certainly have the right to say to the United States
"Look, we helped you with the Saddam Hussein issue, now
you join us in settling the Israel issue." The coalition forces
were called together after 9/11 to deal with terror wherever
it existed, and nowhere is terror more pronounced than in
Israel.

When asked " what shall be the signs of thy coming

and the end of the age?" Jesus responded by expounding to them the signs of the end of this present age. In Luke 21, verses 20-24, we can see this. He first spoke of events to come just four decades after his own death. Jerusalem would be destroyed, the Jews forced to flee, and many would fall by the sword and be taken captive. The next statement is very significant:

> "----and Jerusalem shall be trodden down of the Gentiles, until the times of the Gentiles be fulfilled."

The Occupation of the Land of Palestine, and Jerusalem in particular, (which started in 586 BC with Nebuchadnezzar's invasion of Israel), was to come to an end. Once again armies were to encompass the city. This time they would be known as the "Armies of the Nations." God would gather them there for the express purpose of dealing with the world order and its Mid-East policies that mandates the dividing of the land. The following statistics are interesting as they relate to these multinational forces of prophecy.

MULTINATIONAL FORCES IN PROPHECY

At least forty five times the Bible mentions Multinational forces, called the "Armies of the Nations," or a similar title. In Chapter 2 we introduced this subject. Let us enlarge upon it a little more at this time.

Forty-three of the forty-five references are directly associated with the last days. All but eight are directly related to situations involving the re-gathering of Israel and problems over Jerusalem. Nineteen, or nearly one-half, show that the introduction of these Multi-national forces will begin with an invasion of Babylon, or present day Iraq. Seventeen of the forty-five show them gathering around Jerusalem proper.

According to the prophetic texts of Scripture, I think there can be no question about the involvement of these world armies in the Middle East in the last days. Nor can there be any doubt as to their purpose and intent. They will represent a World Order, as it steps in to force it's will upon the area. Their involvement in the Middle East would begin with problems over Iraq, or old Babylon, then escalate to the whole area involved in the territory of the terrorist nations as enumerated in Ezekiel 32. Thus they must eventually get involved with the Palestinian/Israel border problem, and be used of God to "plead" for Israel because of the divided land (Joel 3:1-2).

The "Dragon," giving the World Order its *"power, seat, and great authority"* (Revelation 13:2) and using the world authority (namely the UN or a future counterpart) will force issues upon the area which go contrary to God's prophetic plan. Again, as Mr. Joseph de Coursey Jr. has said: "what is happening in the Middle East is going to bring the world to its last battle."

When we review the references about that last battle in the Scriptures, we are all the more convinced. In Revelation 16:14-16, from which text we get the very word

ARMAGEDDON, we see Devil spirits calling the *"whole world, to gather them to the battle of that great day..."*. This will be the final confrontation between the Lord and his Angels and the Devil's forces drummed up on Earth by *"Principalities and Powers, rulers of the darkness of this age, spiritual wickedness in high places."* (Ephesians 6:12). As we have shown before, prior to that time, the Armies of the Nations will assemble in the valley known as "Jehoshaphat," an area at the upper end of the Kedron Valley just North and East of Jerusalem (Joel 3:2). It is called The Valley of Bareca (Blessing) today. It is scheduled to happen in the days when the Lord has again called the *"captivity of Judah and Jerusalem"* from out of Diaspora where they have been scattered since Jerusalem's capture, as the Lord said in Luke 21:24. In Joel chapter 3, God says: *"I will also gather all nations..."* and *"will plead with them there for my people and for my heritage Israel, whom they have scattered among the nations..."* Note this next statement: *"and parted my land"* (Joel 3:2). Read verses 11-17 of Joel 3 for the outcome of that battle. A great assembly of Gentile forces will be gathered to "prepare war." *"Multitudes, Multitudes in the valley of decision"* (v.14). "There will I sit to judge all the nations round about (Jerusalem). I believe great victory to follow; what is called in Revelation, the Battle of Armegeddon. For *"the day of the Lord is near in the valley of decision"*(v.14). After that great victory, the final outcome of the Armies of the Nations gathered in the Middle East, we read in verse 16:

The Lord shall roar out of Zion, and utter his voice from
Jerusalem; and the heavens and the earth shall shake; but
the Lord will be the hope of his people, and the strength of
the children of Israel. So shall ye know that I am the Lord
your God dwelling in Zion, my holy mountain; then shall
Jerusalem be holy... (v.16)

The next few verses of the chapter are clearly
Millennial in content. PTL.

Zephaniah 3:8 agrees:

For my determination is to gather the nations, that I may
assemble the kingdoms, to pour upon them mine indig-
nation, even all my fierce anger.

A World Order, preparing a final thrust, and determined to bring Israel into full compliance with its own
political aims, will send its "peace-keeping forces" there. I
have been using what influence I have to warn our government not to send troops into Israel, but America is a
strong part of the Multi-national Forces. It can spell disaster for our troops. Any soldier, conscientious of these
things, should refuse to serve in any campaign that
involves Israel. Our military aims for peace-keeping can
be honored by all, and our personnel held in highest
esteem. Every soldier should serve with distinction, and
honor our Country and Constitution, but when it comes
to being involved with Jerusalem, he or she should be a

conscientious objector. Zechariah 12:2 and 14:2 gives clear warning that "Jerusalem (will be) a burdensome stone for all people" and "a cup of trembling to all nations round about" and:

> ...all that burden themselves with it (Jerusalem) shall be cut in pieces, though all the people of the earth be gathered together against it (Zechariah 12:3).

At some point, Russia will decide that the United States and it's peace-keeping forces are not representing her interests in the Middle East. Together with the Balkans, East Germany, Iran, Libya and Ethiopia, Russia will come down against Israel. Because the Mountains of Israel are particularly mentioned in that invasion, (see Ezekiel 38,39), Russia's problem will probably concern the West Bank territories and the dividing of the land (see comments on Ezekiel 35 and 36 in the 2nd chapter).

Whatever the exact scenario, it is evident both from Bible prophecy and the present world scene, that the greatest event in human history is about to commence. The final end of God's promised redemption for Israel, the Church, and the Earth is upon us. In the midst of this present situation, we find direct reference to the Lord's coming (Zechariah 14:4 and others).

THE JERUSALEM PARADOX

Let's examine more closely the prophetic landscape around these events. Recently a national publication

said, "something sinister is happening in the land of
Israel." When we view the present day events in the
Middle East this proves to be true. We know the "sinis-
ter" happenings are being strongly influenced by Hell and
its hate toward God, His people and His plan for the
Land, the Holy Mount, the city and the people of Israel.

Just a few months ago, Jerusalem was considered
untouchable by the Jewish people in Israel. Both the
Jewish Faithful and the Government of Israel held that
Jerusalem was not negotiable. None-the-less, we saw
Rabin guarantee Jordan's continued control over the
Temple Mount and promise to lay Jerusalem on the negotiating table. That city, so gloriously liberated from
Gentile control in 1967, after 2500 years of occupation,
became the joy of all dispersed Jews in the world, as well
as all of Evangelical Christianity. No one would have
dared suggest that that city be divided again or be up for
grabs. Yet here, in Israel's finest hour, a liberal secular
government, willing to compromise anything for political
advantage, is sowing those very seeds of division again.

One tour guide said recently that Israel's greatest mis-
take was to agree to sovereignty for the Arab people over
the Temple Mount. Why Mr. Rabin would give the
Temple Mount into the control of the WAKF voluntarily
is baffling to most faithful Jews, as well as to us
Christians. The WAKF is the Muslim Religious Trust,
ruled by the King of Jordan, and is in charge of the Mount

today. The Temple Mount has been the center of Jewish yearning for 2000 years. "Next year Jerusalem" has echoed in the ears of Jewish children in every part of the world. Now, by Mr. Rabin's commitment to King Hussein of Jordan, it seems an irreversible policy that the Temple Mount be assigned to Jordan.

The Temple Mount holds the key to the heart of Israel. It also holds the key to the entire bulk of prophetic scriptures, but there can be no doubt of its involvement in a coming battle. On the one hand, we read in Ezekiel 5:5, *"Jerusalem, I have set it in the midst of the nations."* On the other hand we read in Zechariah 14:2:

> *And the city shall be taken, and the houses rifled, and the women ravished ; and half of the city shall go into captivity, and the residue of the people shall not be cut off from the city.*

I think it is evident that the city will again be divided.

It is noteworthy in this prophecy that the city is slated to be divided in half. It is not hard for us to relate to a divided city. At the end of the 1948 War of Independence, Jordanian forces captured the Old City of Jerusalem, leaving Western Jerusalem in the State of Israel. From 1948 to 1967, the city was divided in half. Since Israel's recapture of the Old City, Jerusalem "united and whole" has been counted as one city. However, it is the Old City, the Eastern part, called "East Jerusalem,"

that is the point of controversy with the Palestinian people. The present peace negotiations are certainly setting
the stage for a divided city. Any war generated over the
city today would certainly cause the Eastern half to fall,
thus fulfilling the above prophetic scenario. That very
uprising could well happen around the negotiations taking place at present.

As terrorism continues to grow more violent in Israel,
and the situation escalates into an acute and dangerous
situation for the whole world, more and more pressure
will be brought on Israel to compromise its stand on
Jerusalem and the Temple Mount. The Vatican has
already suggested the internationalization of Jerusalem
and making them to be overseers of a commission made
up of all interested parties. The UN's unique position
over the city speaks volumes. It has called Jerusalem
"Corpus Septrium,"(i.e. a body separated). By this they
indicate that Jerusalem is one body, and the world another. This indicates that Jerusalem should be a body separate, much like Washington D.C. was meant to be in its
inception. A city belonging to no one in particular, but
owned by everyone collectively and administered by the
world body politics, (i.e. the UN).

Ehud Omart, Ex-Mayor of Jerusalem has suggested
that Jerusalem be owned by no one, but that its ownership should be ascribed to God himself. And that, under
God, a generic administration be set up of Christian, Jew,

and Muslim counterparts, appointed by the respective groups, to care for the day to day operations. This would of course take it out of the hands of all nations, including the UN. It is not likely that the world will be willing to recognize God's existence or rights in the matter. Certainly the Muslims would object unless that God was Allah. Of course, such an arrangement would be highly offensive to the Jews and Christians. The internationalizing of the city is more likely to happen. To such an end, the prophecies lend themselves nicely. We shall see as we continue.

Let's follow a blow by blow description of this last day battle over Jerusalem, and the consequential intervention of the Lord into that battle. We will study verse by verse the 12th and 14th chapters of Zechariah.

JERUSALEM A BURDENSOME STONE

Let's start with the first verse of Zechariah chapter 12:

The burden of the word of the Lord for Israel, saith the Lord, which stretcheth forth the heavens, and layeth the foundation of the earth, and formeth the spirit of man within him. Behold, I will make Jerusalem a cup of trembling unto all the people round about, when they shall be in the siege both against Judah and against Jerusalem.

The burden of the passage is "for Israel." A burden is a heavy prophecy. Here, God's burden is for Israel and the Promise. The Creator God gives us a picture of a world so shaken, it is likened to a cup in a trembling hand, its contents spilling over because of the shaking. So it is called "a cup of trembling." It is a cup of trembling to, *"all nations round about."*

Today, the nations around Israel are eager to find peace, but powerful influences in the Muslim world, as well as among rougue nations elsewhere are making things extremely hazardous. Saudi Arabia, Iran, and Iraq, with some backing from Russia, are supporting such revolutionaries as Arafat. This is causing a very volatile situation. Not only is Jerusalem becoming a cup of trembling to the nations immediately around her, but she has become, *"a burdensome stone to all people."*

Jerusalem is a real problem to the rest of the world as well.. No one seems to be able to negotiate its status to the satisfaction of everyone involved. Again this is an amazing prophecy. Such a scenario could not have been imagined a half century ago. At the turn of the century, Jerusalem lay in waste much as it had for thousands of years, hardly more than a heap of ruin from over a score or more of destroyed cities. Certainly not of any significance as to warrant world attention. Also, it is an unproductive area with regards to industry and mineral wealth, having no oil or mining industry.

How could such a desolate place be of any consequence to the world? God has excellent foreseeing eyes. Had the diplomats of our world been more aware of the power of religion, and had they been more atuned to God's word and plan for the area, and less wrapped up in their own agenda, they might even now avoid many pitfalls.

Here we are again to that solemn warning. All who burden themselves with Jerusalem will be, *"cut to pieces."*

There is something so sinister about the situation surrounding Jerusalem in these last days, that any who try to manipulate its status, will be dealt a destructive blow, even though, *"all the people of earth be gathered together against it."*

World planners take comfort in numbers, thinking that it constitutes strength. If all the world supports a policy, and it becomes International Law, surely that should settle the matter. For years the vote of the General Assembly of the United Nations has, with the exception of occasionally the United States and Canada, voted excessively against Israel. Of the past more than 44 votes taken in the Security Council which dealt with the Israeli problem, 42 votes were solidly against Israel, with only the United States and Canada consistently supportive of her. Some of the latest votes have been unanimous with even the U.S and Canada voting negative or abstaining. What we are reading here speaks of that very time when even the United States and Canada will stand with the rest of the world against Jerusalem. I believe this statement in Scripture indicates to us that the United States and Canada will join the rest of the world in a stand against God's plan and the Jewish people's hope for Jerusalem. I also read into this passage that Israel will be uncompromising in its stand to make Jerusalem its capital. We may assume this because, whatever the controversy, God is going to side with Israel, and against the world (verses 4-9).

It seems that the interest of all of the other six divisions of monotheistic religions will not take precedence over the interests of the Jews at that time, for the Lord's definite interest is Judah. Verse 7 says: *"The Lord also shall save the tents of Judah first."* The Catholic Church with its 800 millions world wide, and Islam with its 900 millions, and the Greek Orthodox Church representing all of Asia, the Armenean Church, and of course nominal Christianity, under auspices of the UN, together with Evangelical Christianity, seem to carry no weight in these matters with the Lord during this time. The world government and its "mother of Harlots and abominations of all the earth," (Revelation 17), do not seem to supercede God's rights and claims to the Temple Mount and Jerusalem and His plan for the Sons of Abraham.

"...in the Valley of Megiddon" (Zechariah 12:11), refers to Armageddon.

I am convinced that it is of divine purpose that the valley of Megiddo comes into view at this point. All of this will precipitate Armageddon when The Lord enters the scene (verse 9). At a time when the world community decides to force Israel into its mold and places Jerusalem under its control, and the Jews refuse to yield to its will, Armageddon will come. The United States will be forced to back off. Because Russia stood by and let us beat up on its buddy Saddam, now Russia and the world will tell the United States to back off while they bring Israel into line.

REVIVAL IN ISRAEL

When the Armies of the Nations are surrounding Jerusalem and there is no way out, (Luke 21:24 where "perplexity is 'aporia' meaning 'no way out') a revival will break out in Israel. They will see the Lord. Zechariah 12 tells how they will look upon Him whom they have pierced, and they shall mourn for Him. This same revival is shown in Joel chapter 2. Verse 7 recites their prayer at that time:

Spare thy people, oh Lord, give not thy heritage to reproach, that the heathen should rule over them...

These cries are followed by those famous verses:
I will pour out my spirit upon all flesh... (verse 28).

Although this passage is used to support the latter day outpouring upon the Church in Pentecostal Revival- and rightly so as it was referred to by Peter on the day of Pentecost (Acts 2) it is literally a prophecy foretelling a massive outpouring of the Holy Spirit upon the Jews in their return. It will be the spiritual revival of Israel which was to follow the physical renewal as seen in Ezekiel 37.

Paul said such a revival would come to Israel after the "fullness of the Gentile (i.e. the Church), be come in" (Romans 11:25). Then: *"And so all Israel shall be saved* (v.26). *A fountain shall be opened..."*

This is where verse one of the thirteenth chapter of Zechariah finds us. A fountain of spiritual cleansing will be open in Jerusalem following the crisis described in chapter 12, verses 1-3. As we follow the rest of the chapter we read of that spiritual rebirth that will take place in Jerusalem. All of chapter 13 relates to that revival in Israel.

Now we come to the 14th chapter, and follow the sequence: *"The day of the Lord comes..."*

The chapter opens with this setting, then proceeds to tell of the events in Jerusalem surrounding or just prior to the Lord's appearance. We again return to the earlier situation, where all nations are gathered against Jerusalem (v.2).

We may note again, that it is God himself who has predetermined this gathering , as we have discovered concerning Zephaniah 3:8. (See also Micah 4:1-3.) In our text the Lord said, "I will gather them." It will be the final demise of the whole Gentile World System which has ruled the Holy Land and occupied it since Nebuchadnezzer's day. God will deal with them, break their power hold and make way for the coming of Christ and the setting up of the Millennium. It is at this time He will deal with the Beastly System of World Rule. He will also deal with the Antichrist apostate world religious system as it is revealed to us in the book of Revelation. This agrees with verse 3 of our text.

JERUSALEM AGAIN TAKEN AND SACKED

Zechariah Chapter 14, verse 2 reveals a startling dilemma. Jerusalem is once again slated for captivity. It's houses will we rifled, and women ravished. The most revealing fact of the text is:

"...and half of the city shall go forth into captivity, and the residue of the people shall not be cut off from the city."

In the present situation we see the city of Jerusalem divided in half causing great concern in the area. The East side of the city, namely all of Old Jerusalem within the walls, is at present identified with the West Bank. All of West Jerusalem, or the new part of the city, is recognized as a part of Israel proper. It is the Old City, or East Jerusalem, that the PLO and the Palestinian Authority is claiming as it's capitol. In any armed conflict it is possible that the East half of the city would again be taken. Knowing the violent nature of the PLO (as has already been observed by the author himself, during their reign of terror in Lebanon in the late 70's and early 80's) verse 2 is a very real possibility, maybe a very real probability. Although the State of Israel has been officially recognized, it's right to East Jerusalem is not clear, and certainly it's authority to determine control over the Temple Mount is in question.

It is clear to the author that in any armed conflict in the area, the World Community would clearly back Israel's right to exist, but it is doubtful that Israel would find backing in defense of East Jerusalem. Seeing how the UN "peace keeping forces " stood by and watched the rape of Lebanon, where cities were "rifled" and women were "ravished," I doubt seriously whether the world community would intervene if the same were to happen to East Jerusalem. Half of the city is very likely doomed to fall into hateful hands again.

There are, however two exciting and encouraging parts to the prophecy and revelation in Zechariah's words. The first is shown in verse 2: "The residue of the people shall not be cut off from the city." Evidently, the world community at that time will internationalize Jerusalem, allowing the people, namely the Jews and Christians, to enter the city. The second and more exciting revelation however, comes to us in verses 3 and 4. Here we see a divided city will be allowed only briefly. The Lord will come and deal with those occupying forces of the Gentile world bringing total deliverance to the city.

LOCAL AND LIMITED NUCLEAR WAR

It is fairly clear to the author from Zechariah 14:12,13 that at least a limited and local nuclear exchange will be necessary to awaken the nations to the gravity of their policy over Jerusalem and the West Bank. The words of this passage can hardly be misunderstood. They describe so perfectly the results of radiation upon the human body, and match what we know from previous examples of exposure to nuclear fusion, that it startles us again at the foreknowledge of our God. There are, in the author's judgment, at least 16 clear references which depict the last day Apocalypse that must describe nuclear exchange. Included are for instance, Joel 2:30,31, ("blood, fire and pillars of smoke"); Isaiah 29:6,7 where a great noise, quaking earth, and nuclear wind will come upon those same nations as described in Zechariah 14 who fight against Jerusalem; Isaiah 24:1 where earth is empty, wasted and turned upside down, "..*earth burned and few men left*," (see 24:19-23, where earth is utterly broken down, moved exceedingly); and 2 Peter 3:10 "...the heavens shall pass away with a great noise, and the elements shall melt with fervent heat, the earth and the works that are therein shall be burned up" etc. It will take such a soul-searching catastrophe to wake up a sinful world. Of course our blessed hope is that the Church, the bride of Christ will be gone by the time these tragedies happen, and a deceived world, looking for some hope will fall into the hands of a devil-possessed leader.

MAN OF PEACE

A united world, determined to manipulate Israel into

it's mold, and with it's Multinational forces clubbing it's way into the Holy Land, will soon meet it's match in the Lord. Under the guise of "peace keeping" a seven year "Covenant" is about to be enacted, which I believe will allow the Jews access to the Mount, and internationalize all the Holy Places in Jerusalem. In a time of severe crisis of near holocaust proportions, there will be a strong man arise out of the occult world with some political standing, who will come to the head of a World Order. Three times the book of Daniel tells us his platform will be peace. However, the deep roots of paganism, propagated through the internationally accepted New Age philosophy and claiming to make men their own God, will be his religion.

Daniel says he will worship the "God of Forces" (i.e. cosmic force), and will worship a strange God which his fathers knew not. The Hebrew word for "force" in this passage, does not refer to a military force but to an inner strength, a fortification of the inner self. It is the Hebrew word "Maoz" which is used mostly as an inner strength of self. If a "military fortress would have been intended, the word would have more likely have been "Cheyil" or "Mibtsar." The word "Maoz" compares well with the New Age awakening of the "divine conscience," "harmonic convergence," or "divinity within" notion of teaching. Self realization, and the cult of "self esteem, taught even by many "Christian' clergy, fit nicely into the spirit of inner strength. I fear such teaching is bordering dangerously close to the spirit of Anti-christ as shown here in Daniel.

With this philosophy he will be easy prey for Satan, the God of self, who will incarnate him and convince him that he is God (II Thessalonians 2:4). He will have "indignation against the Covenant" (Daniel 11:30), and will break the Covenant in the middle of the 7 years (Daniel 9:27), setting himself up as God in the Temple, which will be built by that time.

Here is the "Abomination of Desolation, spoken of by Daniel" mentioned by our Lord in Matthew 24:15. Thus, by Jesus' admonition, the faithful Jews will flee into the wilderness, where they will be kept by God's protection for *"time, times and half a time,* (i.e. 3 1/2 years) *from the face of the serpent"* (Revelation 12:14). Through mighty plagues and pestilences, (Revelation 15-16) the Lord will weaken the International System known as the Beast, and his False Prophet, and will bring complete deliverance to Israel and the Church.

ISRAEL AND THE CHURCH- TWO INSTRUMENTS OF SALVATION ON THE EARTH

After the Tribulation time, as revealed in Zechariah 14:12-14 and the setting up of the millennial reign of the Lord (verses 4-11), we find Israel and the Church working together as instruments of salvation and blessing to the whole world (verses 16-21). The Church throughout the nations will go up each year to celebrate with the Jews at the "Feast of Tabernacles" in Jerusalem. By this time the Jewish people will have accepted their Messiah as being who He is, even our Lord and Savior Jesus Christ, for they will meet Him at His coming into Jerusalem from the Mount of Olivet, (v. 4) with the cry *"Blessed be he that comes in the name of the Lord"* (Matthew 23:39).

I was careful not to expose one of our guides or embarrass him before the group, so I waited for a private moment to ask him about his conviction about the Christ of the Christians possibly being the Messiah of the Jews. His response was interesting, and probably reflective of a secretly common attitude in Israel. After a moment of reflection he said, "When the Messiah comes, I will ask him 'have you ever been here before?'" Another Guide confided in me, "If your Jesus turns out to be my Messiah, I will gladly serve him." It is a thrill to anticipate the day when many in Israel will welcome Him home by crying, as Jesus prophesied, "Blessed be he that comes in the name of the Lord."

This all agrees perfectly with James' prediction found in Acts 15:13-16. We see from Romans 11 how the first organ of salvation, namely Israel, would be cut off. There would be "blindness in part" until the fullness of the Gentiles be brought in. Then, according to both Romans and Acts 15, after God has "visited the Gentiles to take out of them a people for his name," the Lord would then:

"return and will build again the tabernacle of David, which is fallen down" (verse 14). It will be built from its "ruins" for the purpose:

> *"that the residue of men might seek after the Lord, and the Gentiles upon whom my name is called,* (the Church), *saith the Lord, who doeth all these things"* (verse 17).

With both Israel and the Church recognizing Jesus as Messiah and Lord, there will be a mutual effort to exalt him and worship him from out of Jerusalem.

Because of recent events in America, it is evident that the Church is a powerful factor in the world. The non-religious minority might as well get used to the idea that the Church and the faithful Jews are going to play a very powerful role in the world. And frankly, after seeing the mess that has and is being made by that minority, I think this nation and the world is about ready to welcome that role. After a rebellious faction in the world has been dealt with by the Lord, the rest of the world will welcome King Jesus. The Jews, together with the Christians are going to play a great part in that welcome.

When asked by a reporter if he and Israel felt "isolation in the world," Mr. Rabin answered boldly:

> "Not at all, because we have millions of Christians praying for us and supporting us. We are not alone."

Add to this the great support of the promises of God and His direct promise of intervention, and they certainly should not feel isolated.

In verses 4-11 of Zechariah 14, we have some most startling and exciting revelations which supports the hope of both Israel and the Church. Right in the middle of the world's best plans for the future of Jerusalem and the Jewish state, we read: *"And his feet* (The Lord's) *shall stand in that day up on the mount of Olives,..."* And: *"The Lord my God shall come, and all the saints with thee."* And again: *"Living waters shall go out of Jerusalem...."* And again: *"And the Lord shall be king over all the earth; in that day shall there be one Lord, and his name one."* And finally: *"and there shall be no more utter destruction; but Jerusalem shall be safely inhabited."*

Beloved friends, the harvest is about over (Jeremiah 8:20). The "times of the Gentiles" is about "fulfilled." the "fullness of the Gentiles" is about to come in.   God is turning again to His ancient land and people.

And this Gospel of the Kingdom shall be preached in all
the world for a witness and then shall the end come
(Matthew 24:14).

In November of 2001, just after the 9/11 crisis, Linda Stoufer made an exciting statement on CNN. While revealing the number of participants in the great religions of the world and their distribution, Linda suddenly gave a startling statistic. She said:

"We now have, for the first time in history, a universal religion. Christianity is now in every nation of the world."

Surely the harvest is nearly over. The time is at hand. Are you saved? Is Christ both your Lord and Savior, or will you have to say with those left behind, as in Jeremiah 8:20:

"The harvest is past, the summer is ended, and we are not saved."

Come to the Savior today, friends, for the day of Grace is soon to be over, and the days of the vengeance of our God is about upon us. All of the events in the world, and especially those in the Middle East prove it to be so.

In the name of the Lord, whom I serve, and whom we seek to glorify in these writings, I leave you to decide. AMEN!